SCOTTISH NAMES

Gordon Jarvie

Chambers

Published 1992 by W & R Chambers Ltd,
43–45 Annandale Street, Edinburgh EH7 4AZ

British Library Cataloguing in Publication Data

A catalogue record for this book is available from the
British Library.

ISBN 0–550–20069–X

Acknowledgments

No student of Scottish surnames can fail to acknowledge the
authoritative work on the subject, *The Surnames of Scotland*, by
George F. Black, published by the New York Public Library
(1946). Almost half a century after its first appearance, this book
remains the 'last word'. Acknowledgment is also made to
The Scotsman and the Registrar General for the lists given in the
introduction.

Cover design by John Marshall

Typeset by Buccleuch Printers Ltd, Hawick
Printed in Singapore by Singapore National Printers Ltd

Contents

Introduction

This is a reference book of Scottish names organized in two alphabetical sections: (1) first names, and (2) surnames. These two aspects of nomenclature are not normally combined in a single reference book, which is a pity. The advantage of combining them within a single volume is to provide the reader with a better historical overview of the evolution of Scottish names, from a period when it was customary for people to have only one name, through to the period (in Scotland the 12th century) when surnames first started to be used and recorded.

It is possible in this book to examine names which have gone the full circle from a Christian name to a surname in the 12th century, and back again to a first name in the 19th or 20th centuries. Look, for example, at medieval Wil (diminutive of William), giving surname Wilson by the 15th century, which then crops up as an occasional forename in the 20th century. Or Christian name Richard, giving the surname Ritchie, also found as an occasional forename in the 20th century.

First Names

Many Scottish first names have close similarities with those in use elsewhere in the English-speaking world, and indeed more generally in the Christian countries of Europe. Yet the names used in Scotland have their own resonances which reflect Scotland's history and geography. With seven kings called James in Scotland and eight called Henry in England, it is natural that these two common Christian names should have a different impact north and south of the border, even today. The use of Ailsa, Iona, Isla, Lorne, Merrick and Morvern as first names – they are all Scottish placenames – is unlikely to mean quite the same outside Scotland as within. Outsiders may know the names of Scottish saints – notably of Columba, Mungo, Margaret and Ninian – but they cannot revere them in quite the same way as native Scots. Scottish surnames – such as Campbell, Gordon, Menzies, Fraser – are a rich source of first names. But, whereas non-Scots probably only use them because they like the sound of them, Scots use them for a more complex variety of cultural reasons – they may be maternal surnames, or surnames of other more distant kin, or they may be traditional in a certain family.

This book tries to include all first names that have a special Scottish resonance, that feature in history, or that have a special following in Scotland. Names are omitted – like Jeremy, Pamela, or Sally – if there is nothing specially Scottish to say about them. This is a slightly subjective basis for exclusion or inclusion, but a national consciousness is itself a subjective thing.

Scotland's other language is of course Gaelic, so wherever possible Gaelic equivalents are indicated.

Surnames

Scottish surnames date from around the 12th century, and come from four main sources. They are:

- *patronymics* – formed by the father's Christian name and adding the suffix *son* (if it was an English name), or the prefix *Mac* (if it was a Gaelic name), eg Donaldson, Farquharson, Nicolson, MacArthur, MacNeil, MacRobbie:

- *local or territorial names* – Fyfe, Murray, Peebles, Sutherland; or Craig, Lochhead, Muir;

- *occupational names* – Forrester, Hunter, Mason, Wright;

- *nicknames* – Auld, Brown, Lang, Younger; or MacIldowie, MacIlraith, MacIlroy ('son of the black lad', 'son of the freckled lad', 'son of the red-haired lad', respectively).

It will be noted that a disproportionately large number of Scottish surnames are from Norman–French sources (Bruce, Cumming, Fraser, Grant, Lindsay, Melville, Sinclair, etc). This is mainly because the Norman influx into Scotland coincided exactly with the period when surnames were coming into general use.

Many of the surname entries in this book make mention of a family name recorded in 1296, or even of a person who did homage in 1296. This is a reference to a document of the summer of that year, popularly referred to as the *Ragman Roll*, which was extorted by King Edward I of England in the course of a military progress through Scotland as evidence of his subjugation of the Scots. The same expedition removed the Stone of Destiny to London. The *Ragman Roll* is a list of the nobility, landowners and burgesses of the Scottish Lowlands in that year, and is more comprehensive than most charters, witness lists, petitions, letters of denization (or citizenship) and other papers of the period which yield information to us about the origins and development of Scots surnames.

Generally, the book concentrates on names that still feature in telephone directories. Obsolete names, however interesting their etymologies, are ignored.

There is no Scottish double-barrel tendency, as in England, outside the ranks of the aristocracy. Instead there is the two-part surname, with no hyphens involved, in which usually only the final surname passes to the children. Examples are John Logie Baird, James Keir Hardie, James Ramsay MacDonald, Anne Lorne Gillies, Allan Campbell MacLean, George Mackay Brown, Iain Crichton Smith. Double forenames are also quite common in the Highlands, eg Alan John MacCallum: this was a means of distinguishing an individual in a family with more than one Alan MacCallum.

Cross-Referencing

Names in bold type within entries cross-refer the reader to other entries for further information. Remember when checking a cross-reference that the book is in *two* sections – first names and surnames – and that the cross-reference may be in either.

The 10 most popular boys' and girls' names in Scotland, 1990

(according to the birth columns of *The Scotsman*, with number of mentions in brackets)

1	Andrew (47)	1	Sarah (36)
2	Christopher (32)	2	Rebecca (25)
3	Callum (31)	3	Fiona (24)
4	James (31)	4	Emma (23)
5	David (28)	5	Kirsty (23)
6	Euan (26)	6	Katherine (21)
7	Michael (25)	7	Hannah (18)
8	Alastair (24)	8	Catriona (17)
9	Ross (21)	9	Jennifer (17)
10	Stuart (21)	10	Laura (16)

Names which dropped out of *The Scotsman* top 10 between 1989 and 1990: Alison, Eilidh and Matthew.

The 20 commonest surnames in Scotland

(based on lists compiled by the Registrar General Scotland for 1990)

1	Smith	11	Johnston/Johnstone
2	Brown	12	Murray
3	MacDonald/ McDonald	13	Reid
		14	Taylor
4	Wilson	15	Mackay/MacKay
5	Stewart	16	MacKenzie/ McKenzie
6	Thomson		
7	Campbell	17	Clark
8	Robertson	18	Young
9	Anderson	19	MacLean/McLean
10	Scott	20	Ross

FIRST NAMES

Adam (*m.*)
Gaelic **Adhamh**
A popular personal name in Scotland from early times. The word derives from the Hebrew for man, and the red soil from which God created him. Adamnan ('little Adam') was the biographer of St Columba in the seventh century.

Aeneas (*m.*)
A transliteration of Gaelic Aonghas. (See also **Angus**.)

Agnes (*f.*)
Gaelic **Aigneas**
The Latin version of a Greek word meaning 'chaste', popular in Scotland in the 19th century. Associated with the patriotic achievements of 'Black Agnes' at Dunbar Castle in the 14th century, popularized in Sir Walter Scott's *Tales of a Grandfather* (1827–9). Popular diminutives have included Aggie and **Nessie**. The reverse form **Senga** is also found.

Aidan (*m.*)
Gaelic **Eadan**
The name of a king of Dalriada (died 606) and of a saint (died 651) who went from Iona to become abbot of Lindisfarne. Now more widespread in Ireland than in Scotland.

Aiken, **Aitken** (*m.*)
A forename from a surname. Perhaps in use as a first name as a result of the children's rhyme 'Aiken Drum'.

> There cam a man tae oor toon,
> Tae oor toon, tae oor toon;
> There cam a man tae oor toon
> An' they ca'd him Aiken Drum.

1

> He played upon a ladle,
> A ladle, a ladle;
> He played upon a ladle
> An' his name was Aiken Drum.

Aileen (f.)
Gaelic **Eibhlin**
Like **Eileen**, this is a version of **Helen**, from Greek meaning 'bright one'. The Gaelic version may derive from Germanic Avelina, which gives **Evelyn**. (See also **Eveline** and **Helen**.)

Ailie (f.)
Gaelic **Ailidh** and **Ailis**
A Scottish form of **Alice**, sometimes confused with **Eilidh**, the Gaelic form of **Helen**.

Ailsa (f.)
A borrowing from Ailsa Craig, the rocky islet in the Firth of Clyde. The actress Ellen Terry is quoted as saying: 'Ailsa Craig! What a magnificent name for an actress!'

Ainslie (m.)
A surname in use as a first name. The surname probably derives from the English placename Annesley, in Nottinghamshire.

Aithne see Eithne.

Alasdair (m.)
The Gaelic name for **Alexander**. Other spellings include Alistair, Alastair, Alister, etc. Diminutives are Ally and in Gaelic Aili, Ailig and Sandaidh.

Alexander (m.)
Gaelic **Alasdair**
Greek name for the defender of men, given to Paris in the *Iliad* and to the kings of Macedonia, including Alexander the Great. Queen Margaret introduced the name into Scotland, her son becoming King Alexander I. By the reigns of Kings Alexander II and III in the 13th century, the name had become widespread in Scotland. Diminutives are Alec, Alex, Ally, **Sandy**, Sawney. The female form is Alexandra.

2

Alice (*f.*)
Gaelic **Ailidh/Aileas**
The name is from an Old German word for 'nobility', and may have found favour in Scotland as a sort of feminine version of Alex. The diminutive version Alison (Gaelic Allasan) is more popular in Scotland than the original. Alison is often shortened to Ally.

Andrew (*m.*)
Gaelic **Anndra/Aindrea**
From the Greek for 'manly', this is one of Scotland's most popular first names. The apostle Andrew has been Scotland's patron saint since the 13th century. Diminutives include Andy, Dandy and Drew. The feminine form is Andrea and its variants (Andrena, Andrewina, Dreena, Rena).

Angus (*m.*)
Gaelic **Aonghas**
The Gaelic word means 'unique choice' and a nobleman of this name is commemorated in the Angus district of Tayside. Aeneas is sometimes associated with it. The shortened version is Gus.

Archibald (*m.*)
Originally a Germanic name meaning 'bold' and 'true', the name has also been used as a translation of Gaelic Gilleasbuig, where *gille* means 'shaven or bald servant or follower'. The name was especially popular with the **Douglas** and **Campbell** clans, as in Archibald Douglas, nicknamed 'Bell-the-Cat' (5th Earl of Angus, *c.*1449–1514) in memory of his courage – as a mere 'mouse' – in putting a bell round the neck of the 'cat' (a dangerous royal favourite). Shortened forms of the name are Archie and (Gaelic) **Eàirdsidh**.

Athol, Atholl (*m.*)
A district of Perthshire which gave rise to a surname now also occasionally in use as a first name. Athol Fugard is a South African playwright.

Barry, Barrie (*m.*)
A surname which has become a popular first name in Scotland, Ireland and North America (Kevin Barry, Barry Goldwater). It may derive from various place-names, including a village in Angus.

Beth (*f.*)
Like **Elspeth**, a popular Scottish variant of **Elizabeth**.

Betty (*f.*)
Gaelic **Beitidh**
A diminutive of **Elizabeth**/Ealasaid, derived from Elisheba (Hebrew for 'oath of God').

Blair (*m.*)
Gaelic **Blar**
A surname now also used as a first name. Blair is also a location (Blair Athol, Blairgowrie, etc), *blar* in Gaelic meaning 'a plain'.

Brenda (*f.*)
From an Old Norse name Brand, meaning 'sword', long in use in Shetland. Popularized by the heroine of Sir Walter Scott's novel *The Pirate* (1821).

Brian (*m.*)
A Gaelic form of Breannan, or Brendan. Brian Boru was an Irish warrior king in the 11th century. The spelling Bryan is also found.

Bruce (*m.*)
Gaelic **Brus**
A Scottish surname in common use as a first name since about 1930. The pet form Brucie has been popularized by the TV personality Bruce Forsyth.

Bryce, **Brice** (*m.*)
A surname and a Christian name in Scotland from the 12th century. There was a Gaulish St Bricius, said to be the 'grumpy saint', so the forename is also found in France.

Cairns (*m.*)
A surname and a personal name, probably from the district of Cairns (Midcalder, Midlothian).

Caleb (*m.*)
From a Hebrew word meaning 'intrepid', perhaps popular in Scotland for its biblical cadence. Not common nowadays.

Calum (*m.*)
The Scots Gaelic form of Irish Colm, from Latin *columba* ('a dove'). *Columba* in Scots Gaelic is *Calum Cille* ('the dove of the Church'). Columba was the Irish missionary who established Christianity at Iona and effected the conversion of the Scots and the Picts. He was the most revered saint among Scots. A derived name was MaolCholuim, 'the follower of Calum', giving **Malcolm**.

Cameron (*m.*)
Gaelic **Camran**
A surname now also in regular use as a first name. The forename was perhaps popularized among the Covenanters, or Reformed Presbyterians, who were also known as the Cameronians after one of their popular leaders, Richard Cameron (executed 1680).

Campbell (*m.*)
Gaelic **Caimbeul**
A clan name from Argyll now also in use as a first name.

Carrick (*m.*)
A surname from the district in south Ayrshire, now also found as a first name.

Catherine, Katherine (*f.*)
Gaelic **Catrìona**
Although this is not a particularly Scottish name, it has long been popular and several of its diminutives strike a Scottish note such as **Kate** (Gaelic Ceit), Katie (Ceitidh) and Kathy.

Catriona (*f.*)
Gaelic **Catrìona**
A Gaelic name derived, like **Catherine**, from the Greek word for 'pure'. Twelfth-century crusaders brought back to Europe the legend of the martyred Egyptian princess St Katherine of Alexandria (fourth century), and this spread the name. So did the followers of St Catherine of Siena whose order had a house in Edinburgh (in the district now called Sciennes). Robert Louis Stevenson's novel *Catriona* (1893), the sequel to *Kidnapped* (1886), was a further boost to the name.

5

Charles (m.)
Gaelic **Teàrlach**

From the Old German name for 'man'. It became a royal name of the Stewarts in the 17th century, popularized in Scotland by the exploits of Bonnie Prince Charlie in the 1745 rebellion. Gaelic Teàrlach has the same pronunciation as Charlie, and means 'shaped like Thor', the Norse god of war. Feminine forms Charlene and possibly Arleen have also been popular.

Christine (f.)
Gaelic **Cairistìona**

From Latin Christina, a follower of Christ. It was the name of an early Roman martyr and was introduced into Scotland by Queen Margaret in the 11th century. Chrissie (Gaelic Criosaidh) and **Kirsty** (Gaelic Ciorstaidh or Ciorstag) are also popular. Christian is also found, for boys and girls.

Clair, Clare (f.)
Gaelic **Sorcha**

The English name is from Latin for 'clear', and the Gaelic name with which it is associated means 'bright'. Derivatives include Clarissa, and Robert Burns's beloved Clarinda, 'mistress of my soul'. The name was spread throughout Europe in the Middle Ages by the religious order of the Sisters of St Clara, the 'Poor Clares'.

Clark (m.)
From a surname recorded in Scotland from the 12th century. Perhaps popularized as a first name by the filmstar Clark Gable.

Cochrane (m.)
From lands near Paisley, in Renfrewshire. Thomas Cochrane 'the liberator' of Chile and Peru, 10th Earl of Dundonald (1775–1860), was probably the most illustrious bearer of the surname, and may have popularized its use as an occasional first name.

Coinneach (m.)
A popular Gaelic name, meaning 'fair one' and sometimes taken as the equivalent of **Kenneth**. For example, Coinneach Mac Alpin (died 858), first king of the united Scottish and Pictish lands, is generally translated as Kenneth MacAlpine.

6

Colin (m.)
Gaelic **Cailean**
The English name is from an Old French derivative of Nicolas, while the Gaelic is from a word meaning 'cub, or youth'. Much more popular in Scotland than in other English-speaking countries.

Colum (m.)
A variant of **Calum**, from the same source as Columba, the early Christian saint. More widespread in Ireland than in Scotland.

Cormac, Cormack (m.)
Gaelic **Cormag**
The name of a brother of St Columba. His missions took him to the north of Scotland and Orkney. The surname **MacCormack** (MacCormick, MacCormaig) derives from this source. The name itself means 'a charioteer'.

Cosmo (m.)
A rare name, from Greek 'an ordered system' (cosmos, cosmic). The name was popularized in 18th-century Scotland by Cosmo George, 3rd Duke of Gordon (died 1752). Cosmo Lang (1864–1945) was a Scottish-born archbishop of Canterbury.

Craig (m.)
From the Gaelic word *creag*, 'a rock'. A common Scots surname also popular as a first name.

Crawford (m.)
A placename in upper Clydesdale which yielded a surname. The surname in turn is now used as a first name. The governess of Queen Elizabeth and Princess Margaret, Marion Crawford, was affectionately known as Crawfie by her young charges.

Crichton (m.)
A surname, from the barony of Crichton in Midlothian, which has given rise to an occasional forename. 'The Admirable Crichton' (1560–82), so-called because he was good at everything, enjoyed a popular reputation in the 17th century.

Cuthbert (*m.*)
Gaelic **Cùithbeirt**

The name of the English saint (*c.*635–687) who was bishop of Hexham and of Lindisfarne. He had also been a monk at Old Melrose and had followers in the south of Scotland. Cille Cùithbeirt (Kirkcudbright) is named after him. The name is not now much found.

Daniel (*m.*)
Gaelic **Danaidh**

From Hebrew for 'God has judged', found in steady use over a long period. Danaidh is the Gaelic diminutive of Domhnall, pronounced like and akin to English Danny. Feminine forms Danielle and Daniella are also found.

David (*m.*)
Gaelic **Dàibhidh**

From the Hebrew name of an Old Testament king of Israel, meaning 'beloved'. There were two Scottish kings of this name (1124–53 and 1329–71) which has ensured its continued popularity in Scotland. Surnames **Davidson** and Dawson derive from David.

Deirdre (*f.*)

A Gaelic name, from a tragic heroine of Celtic legend. The bards compared her beauty to that of Helen of Troy. She eloped from Ireland to Scotland with Naois, but later committed suicide after the execution of her lover. Hence 'Deirdre of the sorrows'.

Diarmid, Diarmad (*m.*)

Another Celtic legendary name. Diarmad was one of the Fiann warrior followers of Fionn mac Cumhail (**Fingal**). He was killed hunting a wild boar, and is said to be the progenitor of the clan **Campbell**. The name means 'without envy' and is anglicized as Dermot or Dermid. The surnames **MacDiarmid** and MacDermot derive.

Dollag, Dolag (*f.*)

In common use as a Gaelic name, a feminine version of Domhnall. The English version is Dolina.

Donald (*m.*)
Gaelic **Domhnall**
The Gaelic name means 'world ruler', and it was borne by six early Scots kings. Don and Donnie are shortened versions, and **Donaldson** and **MacDonald** are derived surnames. Donald Duck made the name popular in America.

Doreen (*f.*)
A mainly Irish name, popular in Scotland in the first half of the 20th century. It may be an adaptation of **Dorothy**. A short form is Dorrie.

Dorothy (*f.*)
Gaelic **Dearbhàil/Diorbhàil**
From the Greek meaning 'gift of God'. Popular abbreviations are Dot, Dolly (Gaelic Dollaidh), Dora and Dodie.

Douglas (*m.*)
Gaelic **Dughlas**
A placename and river name in Lanarkshire, meaning 'dark water' in Gaelic. This became a surname around 1200 and a first name from the 17th century. Short forms are Doug and Duggie.

Drummond (*m.*)
A surname from a placename (Blair Drummond, also Drymen which probably has a similar etymology). In occasional use as a first name.

Dugald (*m.*)
Gaelic **Dughall**
The word is from Gaelic *dubh* ('black'), *gäll* ('stranger'). This was the term for a Danish Viking as opposed to a Norwegian one, a *fionghall* or fair stranger. It has given surnames Dougal and **MacDougall**.

Dulcie (*f.*)
From Latin *dulcis* (sweet). More formal derivatives such as Delcine and Dulcinea never caught on in Scotland.

Duncan (*m.*)
Gaelic **Donnchadh**
Derived from the Celtic for 'brown warrior', it was the name of two kings of Scots in the 11th century (one murdered by Macbeth), and of a saint-abbot of Iona (died 717). It is also widespread as a Scots surname.

Eàirdsidh (*m.*)
A shorter version of Gilleasbuig, influenced by the similar-sounding Archie.

Ebenezer (*m.*)
From the Hebrew meaning 'stone of help'. Popular for its Old Testament echoes in the 17th–19th centuries but now rare. Eben and Ebie are shortened forms.

Eileen (*f.*) see **Aileen**.

Eilidh (*f.*)
A diminutive of Eibhlin or **Helen**. Probably also akin to **Elaine** and Ellen. The name has acquired recent popularity outside Gaelic areas where it has long been common.

Eithne (*f.*)
Gaelic for 'a kernel, or grain'. Eithne was the mother of St Columba and several saints bore the name.

Elaine, Ellen (*f.*)
Gaelic **Eibhlin/Eilidh**
Older forms of **Helen**, from Old French Hélène. This in turn was derived from Greek 'the bright one', a name renowned in literature by the immortal beauty of 'the face that launched a thousand ships' – Helen of Troy. The 'H' was not added to Helen till the 15th century, when Renaissance scholars revived the study of Greek literature. So the name is first found as Elena, then Elaine and Ellen.

Elizabeth (*f.*)
Gaelic **Ealasaid**
From the Hebrew Elisheba, for 'oath of God'. The Christian name spread from Byzantium across Europe in the later Middle Ages, initially in the form

10

of **Isobel**, with which it was interchangeable. Queen Elizabeth of England (1533–1603) popularized the name throughout Britain. Popular Scottish pet forms include Bessy, Beth, Betsy, Betty, Elsie, Elspeth, Liza, Lizbeth and Lizzy. Gaelic pet forms are Beitidh, Liosaidh and Lisidh.

Eliot, Elliot, Elliott (*m.*)
A Border surname now popular as a first name in Scotland and North America. Eliots guarded the Middle Marches of the Scottish Border, they fell at the battle of Flodden (1513), and it was Jane Eliot who wrote 'The Flowers of the Forest'. Inspector Eliot Ness of the American TV series *The Untouchables* may have popularized the name outside Scotland.

Elsie, Elspeth (*f.*) see **Elizabeth**.

Eppie, Effie (*f.*)
Gaelic **Oighrig/Eighrig**
Scots diminutive forms of Euphemia, from Greek 'well spoken of'. One of Robert Burns's inamorata was Eppie Adair, while Effie Deans was one of the heroines of Sir Walter Scott's bestseller *Heart of Midlothian* (1818).

Erskine (*m.*)
A placename in Renfrewshire taken as a Norman Scots family name in the 12th century, and hence a first name which has now spread through the English-speaking world: Erskine May (English jurist), Erskine Childers (Anglo-Irish author of *The Riddle of the Sands*, 1903) and Erskine Caldwell (American author of *Tobacco Road*, 1932).

Eveline, Evelyn, Evlyn (*f.*)
Gaelic **Eibhilin/Eibhlin**
These names are probably akin to **Elaine**, Ellen and **Helen**, and they may also have suggested kinship with Eve. Old Germanic Avelina is a probable source of the names. Evelyn had a vogue in Scotland in the period 1900–30.

11

Ewan (*m.*)
Gaelic **Eòghann**

From the Gaelic for 'well born'. Welsh Owen is probably akin; in some areas it is also associated with **Hugh**. **MacEwen** and MacEwan are derived surnames.

Farquhar (*m.*)
Gaelic **Fearchar**

A common Gaelic Christian name, meaning 'dear one'. A Dalriadic king (died 697) bore the name. Clan **Farquharson** derives from this name, as do surnames **MacFarquhar**, McKerchar and Kerracher.

Fergus (*m.*)
Gaelic **Fearghas**

The Gaelic word means 'supreme choice' and the name was common in Scottish legend and early history. Fearghas 'of the cars' – presumably a charioteer – was in the tales of the Fiann. There was a Pictish saint of this name in the eighth century, and Fearghas Earl of Galloway (died 1161) was a rebel against the Scottish crown. The surname **Ferguson** and placename Ferguslie derive from this name.

Fife, Fyfe (*m.*)

A Scottish region and Pictish kingdom from which is derived a surname and occasional first name. Fyfe Robertson (1902–87), the broadcaster, was a well-known bearer of this name.

Fingal (*m.*)
Gaelic **Fionnghal**

A Gaelic name derived from *fionn* (fair) and *ghal* (stranger), a Norwegian as opposed to a Danish Viking. (**Dugald** was a dark stranger.) There was a Fingal, king of Man and the Hebrides in the 11th century. The name was also revived in the Ossian saga of James MacPherson (1738–96). Fionnghal is an extension of Fionn, and Fionn mac Cumhail – Finn McCool in English – was the great hero of the Celtic tales. Fingal's Cave in Staffa commemorates this hero of Celtic mythology. It is a similar basaltic rock formation to the Giant's Causeway of County Antrim in Ireland, which is also said to have been the work of Fionn mac Cumhail.

Finlay (*m.*)
Gaelic **Fionnlagh**
The Gaelic name means 'fair hero', and was a common first name in the Highlands. It gives rise to the surnames Finlayson and **MacKinlay** (Mac Fionnlagh).

Fiona (*f.*)
This name was invented by the Paisley writer William Sharp (1855–1905), who wrote under the pseudonym Fiona Macleod. His work is long forgotten but the pen-name lives on. The name is based on Gaelic *fionn* ('fair one').

Fletcher (*m.*)
A surname occasionally in use as a first name. Fletcher Christian was the 18th-century ringleader of the mutiny on the *Bounty*, and Marlon Brando's film interpretation popularized the name internationally.

Flora (*f.*)
Gaelic **Floraidh**
From the Roman goddess of flowers and spring, Flora, who derives in turn from Latin *flos*, a flower. Flora Macdonald (1722–90), protectress of Bonnie Prince Charlie, brought the name lasting renown and popularity in Scotland. She occasionally signed her name Florie, which is the Gaelic pronunciation, and this may be the origin of the pet form Florrie. Flossie is another pet form.

Forbes (*m.*)
Gaelic **Foirbeis**
A district of Strathdon in Aberdeenshire, which gave rise to a surname, and later an occasional first name.

Frances (*f.*), **Francis** (*m.*)
Gaelic **Frangag** (*f.*) **Frang** (*m.*)
Derives from Latin *franciscus*, a Frank or Frenchman. St Francis of Assisi (1182–1226) and the Franciscan monastic order spread the appeal of this name throughout Europe by the Renaissance. Frank is popular in Scotland as a male version, being very close to the Gaelic. Fanny and Franny are female pet forms.

Fraser (*m.*)
Gaelic **Friseal**

The Gaelic form is closer to the Old French original, which was Frizel. Frizel was a Norman knight whose descendants acquired land in Buchan and Inverness. The name was from Old French *freze*, a strawberry, and strawberry leaves form part of the armorial bearings of the Frasers/Frisealaich. In time, the Frasers became a Gaelic-speaking clan. The town of Fraserburgh was founded by them.

Gail, Gale, Gael (*f.*)
Short versions of Abigail, popular in Scotland in their own right. This local popularity may derive from the word's Gaelic resonance, though the more formal Abigail is a Hebrew name meaning 'father rejoiced'.

Gary, Garry (*m.*)
The name may have originated from Gaelic Goraidh or from Norse Godrodr, akin to Godfrey and meaning 'God's peace'. Or it may be influenced by the name of the river and glen in Perthshire. Perhaps too it is linked with Welsh Gareth and Irish Garret. The name has been popularized internationally by Gary Cooper, the American filmstar, since the 1930s.

Gavin (*m.*)
Gaelic **Gabhainn**

A popular Scots name since the Middle Ages, from Old German Gawin, meaning a district of land. Gavin Douglas (1474–1522) was a poet and bishop of Dunkeld, famous for his translation of the *Aeneid* into Scots. The Welsh form is Gawayne, from Gwalchmai, 'hawk of the plain'. Sir Gawayne was King Arthur's nephew and a knight of the Round Table.

Gilbert (*m.*)
Gaelic **Gilleabart**

From Old German Giselbert, meaning 'bright pledge'. Formerly a popular Christian name in Scotland. St Gilbert (died 1246) was a bishop of Caithness and founder of Dornoch Cathedral. Diminutives of the name are Gibb and Gibbie, with Gaelic cognates Gibidh and Gioban. Gioban gives surnames **MacGibbon** (MacGiobain), Gibbon and **Gibson** (son of Gioban).

Gillespie (m.)
Gaelic **Gilleasbaig**

The Gaelic means servant (*gille*) of a bishop (*easbaig*), so bearers of the name were originally important church officers. The forename was especially common among the **Campbell**, **Douglas** and **MacDonald** clans.

Note that several popular Christian names used in medieval Scotland began with prefix *gille*, Gaelic for a servant or follower. Added to a saint's name, we get Gilbride (follower of St Brigid), Gilzean (follower of St John), Gilmartin (follower of St Martin), Gilchrist (follower of Christ), and **Gilmour** (follower of the Virgin Mary), etc.

Gilmour (m.)
Gaelic **Gille Mhuire**

The Gaelic name means 'servant of the Virgin Mary'. It was used by officers of the Church, and gave rise to a family name which is now also in occasional use as a first name.

Glen, Glenn (m.)

A modern first name, from the Gaelic word for a narrow valley, *gleann*. It was first popularized in Canada, and the American movie actor Glenn Ford has widened its appeal.

Gordon (m.)
Gaelic **Gòrdan**

A family name from a placename in Berwickshire, meaning a smalll wooded dell. The Gordons became one of the largest and most powerful Scottish clans, and their main power-base was in Aberdeenshire. The heroic death of General Gordon in 1885 at Khartoum made the name popular as a forename.

Grace (f.)
Gaelic **Giorsal**

A name popularized in the 17th century by the Puritans, along with other virtuous names – Faith, Hope, Charity, etc. The name has been specially popular in Scotland.

Graham, Graeme (*m.*)
Gaelic **Greum**
The name of a powerful family in the Scottish Lowlands which rose to prominence in the Wars of Independence. Graham of Claverhouse (1649–89) added lustre and poignancy to the name after Killiecrankie. Its use as a first name is recent. The word is a corruption of Grantham, in Lincolnshire, whence came the first (Norman) Grahams into Scotland.

Grant (*m.*)
Another clan surname which has given a first name. The Norman–French nickname Le Grand meant someone who was tall. The Scots surname dates from the 12th century, but the forename has only been popularized in the 20th. This usage probably began in North America, and may have been influenced by US President Ulysses S. Grant.

Gregor (*m.*)
Gaelic **Greig/Griogair**
From the Greek meaning a watchman, which became Latin *Gregorius*, a common Christian name from the third century. Pope Gregory the Great popularized the name throughout Europe, and the usage Gregor has been popular in Scotland since the Middle Ages but is now less widespread. Greg and Greig are popular short forms. Surnames **MacGregor**, Gregson, **Grierson** and Greer all derive from the name.

Gus see **Angus**.

Guthrie (*m.*)
The name is from Gaelic for a war hero, and the lands of Guthrie are in Forfar district. The placename yields the surname, which in turn gives the occasional, and recent, forename.

Hamilton (*m.*)
A Scottish surname since the 14th century, in occasional use more recently as a first name. Sir Hamilton Harty (1880–1941), the Ulster composer, is an example.

Hamish (*m.*)
Gaelic **Seumas**
Derived from Hebrew Jacob, of uncertain meaning. The name is akin to **James** in English, which is an alternative rendering of Gaelic **Seumas**.

Hazel (*f.*)
One of several plant names which became popular in the 19th century (Daisy, Heather, Iris and Violet are others). Specially popular in Scotland, 1930–70.

Heather (*f.*)
Like Hazel, a plant name that became popular in the late 19th century, especially in Scotland for obvious reasons. The Latin name for heather is *Erica* and this too has become popular.

Hector (*m.*)
Gaelic **Eachann**
The Gaelic name meant 'a horse-lord', and it has long been popularly associated with Hector. Hector was first used in Scotland as an anglicization of the Gaelic name, and it has had a strong hold here since the Middle Ages. Hector Boece (*c.*1465–1536) was a Scots historian and churchman.

Helen (*f.*)
Gaelic **Eibhlin**
From Greek meaning 'the bright one'. The name was popularized by the fourth-century English Saint Helena who at age 80 made a pilgrimage to the Holy Land and is believed to have found the true cross of Christ. The name was first found as **Elaine** or Elena and did not acquire its present spelling till after the Renaissance. The Gaelic name has a possible alternative derivation from Germanic *Avelina*, a hazel nut.

Hugh (*m.*)
An Old Germanic name meaning 'heart' or 'soul'. The Normans spread the name through Britain. In Scotland it was used as a transliteration of various Gaelic names – Aodh, Eoghann and Uisdean. Hughie (or Eoghanan) is a popular diminutive. Scottish surnames Hewitt, Howat, Howatson, **Howie** and Howieson all derive from Hugh. So Jock Howison

who rescued King James I from thugs at Cramond brig in the 15th century is descended from a son of Hugh.

Hunter (*m.*)

A surname from an occupation or activity. There has been a Hunterston in Ayrshire since the time of King Alexander II and the medieval arms of the Hunters of Hunterston bore three hunting horns. An occasional first name.

Ian (*m.*)

Gaelic **Iain**

The Gaelic name for **John**, meaning 'God is gracious'. The name came from the Eastern Church to the rest of Europe with the returning crusaders in the 12th century. Both spellings are popular, with occasional debate about which is the more 'correct'. MacIan is a derived surname.

Innes (*m.*)

From *innis* the Gaelic for island (Inchcape, Inchinnan, Inchkeith), which became a surname and clan name, and is occasionally taken as a first name. The surname **MacInnes** is not related – it means 'son of **Angus**'.

Iona (*f.*)

From a Greek word meaning 'violet-coloured stone'. The girl's name is taken from the island where St Columba established his monastery in 563. (Other island names given to girls are **Ailsa** and **Rona**. Islay is also sometimes found, both for boys and girls.)

Isla (*f.*)

Two Scottish rivers have this name, occasionally found as a girl's name.

Isobel, Ishbel (*f.*)

Gaelic **Iseabail**

From the medieval French Isabelle, whose Hebrew source is Elisheba, meaning 'oath of God', which also gives the name **Elizabeth**. Isa, Ella, Bel and Bella are popular short forms.

Ivor (*m.*)
Gaelic **Iomhair**
A Norse personal name Ivarr, perhaps from Old Norse Ingvar, gives this name in north-east Scotland. The usage is not nearly as widespread as Welsh Ivor/Ifor.

James (*m.*)
Gaelic **Seumas**
From a Hebrew root of uncertain meaning, giving the name Jacob. This became Latin Jacobus or Jacomus. For a long time James was the second most popular boy's name in Scotland (after **John**), with seven Stewart kings taking the name. Jim, Jimmie and Jamie are short forms, all popular in Scotland.

Jane (*f.*)
Gaelic **Sineag**
A feminine form of **John**, from Old French Jehane, long popular in Scotland in both Scots and Gaelic. The Gaelic version anglicizes to **Sheena**.

Janet (*f.*)
Gaelic **Seònaid**
A popular form of **Jane**, widely used in Scotland. The Gaelic version anglicizes as **Shona**.

Janice (*f.*)
A variant of **Janet**, also sometimes spelled Janis.

Jean (*f.*)
Gaelic **Sìne**
Another variant or derivative of **Jane**, which in turn yields the diminutive Jeanette and the pet forms Jenny and Jeannie. 'Bonnie Jean' Armour was the wife of Robert Burns.

Jessie (*f.*)
Gaelic **Seasaid**
In Scotland, this is another diminutive of **Janet** and not associated with Jessica as in England. Very popular in 18th- and 19th-century Scotland.

Joan (f.)
Gaelic **Seonag**

Another feminine form of **John**. An early spelling was Johan, pronounced as two syllables, from which have evolved Johanne, Joanne, Joanna. Gaelic Seonag is a diminutive of **Seònaid**. (See also **Janet**.)

Jock (m.)
Gaelic **Seoc**

A form of **John** popular in Scotland. Scottish soldiers, and by extension all Scotsmen, are sometimes referred to as 'Jocks'. When Scots say they are all derived from the same common stock, they say they are all 'Jock Tamson's bairns'.

John (m.)
Gaelic **Eòin/Iain**

A biblical name from Hebrew meaning 'God is gracious', the name of the apostle and of John the Baptist (Eoin Baisteach). For many centuries, although there were no Scottish kings of this name, John was Scotland's most widely used Christian name, with **Jock** and Jack popular diminutives. Surnames **Johnson** and Jackson derive. (See also **Ian**, a Gaelic cognate.)

Joseph (m.)
Gaelic **Eòsaph**

A favourite and widely used biblical name in Scotland, from Hebrew meaning 'Jehovah increases (the family)'. In the 20th century it has unfortunately tended to acquire a sectarian resonance in some quarters, so its popularity has declined outside Catholic families. The popular diminutive is Jo, as in Jo Grimond (born 1913), the Liberal politician.

Josephine (f.)
The feminine version of **Joseph**, popular in Scotland and Ireland. Pet forms are Jo and Josie.

Julie (f.)
Gaelic **Sìleas**

Julie, like Julia, is a feminine version of Julius, the Roman clan to which Caius Julius Caesar belonged. Italian Giulia reached England as Julia in the 16th century and was popularized by Shakespeare in *Two*

Gentlemen of Verona. In the Highlands, Sìleas na Ceapaich (Sìleas of Keppoch, *c.*1660–1729) was a MacDonald bard resident near Tomintoul, Banffshire. In Scotland, Julie is sometimes given as a 'month name'. (See also **June**.)

June (*f.*)
This is probably the most popular 'month name' in Scottish use. The custom of naming a child by the month of its birth came to Scotland from France at the beginning of the 20th century, and April, Avril, May, Maie and **Julie** are also in use.

Karen (*f.*)
A Danish diminutive of Katherine or **Catherine**, popular in Scotland since the 1930s.

Kate (*f.*)
Gaelic **Ceit**
A shortened version of Katherine or **Catherine**, popular in its own right. Kate Dalrymple is a popular Scottish dance tune named after an 18th-century lady. Kate Kennedy was the daughter of a 15th-century bishop of St Andrews and founder of St Salvator's College there: students still celebrate annually in her name. Katie (Gaelic Ceitidh) is a diminutive.

Katrina (*f.*)
An anglicized spelling of **Catriona**, perhaps influenced by Loch Katrine in the Trossachs.

Kay (*f.*)
A surname deriving from an occupation (a warden, or keeper of a key), now also found as an occasional first name. Sometimes spelled Kaye. Surnames **MacKay** and MacKie have different etymologies.

Keir, Kerr (*m.*)
Gaelic **Ciar**
Surnames (meaning 'a copse') recorded from the 12th century now also in use as first names. Keir Hardy (1856–1915), one of the Scottish founders of the Labour Party, probably popularized the name.

Keith (m.)
Gaelic **Cè**
A Scottish placename from Gaelic 'windy place or wood'. The surname derived from the place and rose to fame with the hereditary earls marischal of Scotland from the 15th century. The forename came into use in the 19th century and remains widely popular.

Kelly (m., f.)
Gaelic **Ceallach**
The Gaelic name was borne by an abbot of Iona in the ninth century and two bishops of St Andrews in the 10th century. Kelly is a common Irish as well as a Scots surname, and there is a Scots variant Kellie from Fife and Angus. The use as a girl's name may date from the marriage of Grace Kelly (1929–82) to Prince Rainier II of Monaco in 1956. The variant Kylie has been popularized in the 1980s and may derive in part from **Kyle**.

Kelvin (m.)
The name of a Scottish river occasionally found as a first name. There may be echoes of Calvin (the religious reformer) in this usage.

Kenneth (m.)
Gaelic **Coinneach**
Kenneth comes from an Old Gaelic name Cined, or 'fire-sprung', but is also used as an anglicization of **Coinneach**, or 'fair one'. Kenneth MacAlpine (died c.860), who united the Scottish and Pictish kingdoms, was probably named after St Coinneach, an assistant of St Columba. Ken and Kenny (Gaelic Ceanag) are short forms.

Kerr (m.)
A Scottish border surname in use as a first name. (See also **Keir**.)

Kevin, Kevan (m.)
Kevin has long been a popular Irish Christian name, after the early saint who founded the monastery at Glendalough, south of Dublin. Kevan is from a Kirkcudbright surname. Kevin is now very popular in Scotland.

Kirsty (*f.*)
Gaelic **Ciorstag**
Popular in its own right in Scotland, though strictly it is a diminutive of **Christine** and Cairistìona.

Knox (*m.*)
A Scottish surname (from Gaelic *cnoc*, 'a hill') occasionally found as a first name. The name acquired special respect after the Reformation, through the fame of John Knox (1513–72).

Kyle (*m.*, *f.*)
A surname from the district of Ayrshire, from the Gaelic word for a narrow strait or channel (Kyles of Bute, Kyle of Lochalsh). Occasionally found as a forename. The diminutive Kylie (*f.*) was popularized in the late 1980s by the Australian TV actress Kylie Minogue.

Lachlan (*m.*)
Gaelic **Lachlann**
The name originally referred to a Norseman, being the Gaelic for 'land of the lochs', ie Scandinavia. Diminutives are Lachie (Gaelic Lachaidh) and Lachann. The surname **MacLachlan** derives.

Laura (*f.*)
The name is a feminine version of **Laurence**, and has been in use throughout Europe since the 12th century. Recent use in Scotland may link it popularly with **Lorna** or **Lorne**.

Laurence, **Lawrence** (*m.*)
Gaelic **Labhrainn**
From Latin *laurus*, a laurel, the symbol of victory. Laurentius (a citizen of Laurentium) was a third-century saint and martyr. The name used to be more popular in Scotland, and survives in placenames Laurencekirk and Lauriston.

Lennox (*m.*)
A surname from the district of Lennox in Dunbartonshire, occasionally found as a first name. Lennox Berkeley (born 1903) is a famous English composer.

Leslie (*m.*), **Lesley** (*f.*)
A surname and clan name from lands in Aberdeen-shire. The girl's name is found nowadays more often than the boy's.

Lewis (*m.*)
Gaelic **Luthais**
In Scotland this name has a special association with the island of Lewis. But the main source of the name is the Old German for 'famous warrior', which also gave Ludwig, Ludovic and Louis. The last spelling is occasionally found, as in Robert Louis Stevenson (1850–94).

Lillias, Lilias (*f.*)
Gaelic **Lili**
These were probably pet forms of **Elizabeth**/Ealasaid, but also associated with the lily flower, a Christian symbol of purity. Lilian and Lily are also found.

Lindsay (*m.*, *f.*)
A forename adopted from a surname and clan name, in turn taken from a Norman–English placename in Lincolnshire. Alternative spellings include Linsey, Lyndsay and Linsay.

Lorna (*f.*)
There were a few Lornas before *Lorna Doone* (1869, in the novel of R. D. Blackmore), but the name became widespread thereafter, especially in Scotland, perhaps because of its closeness to **Lorne**.

Lorne (*m.*, *f.*), **Lorn** (*m.*)
Gaelic **Latharn** (*m.*), **Latharna** (*f.*)
A name adopted from a district of Argyll, after its founder Latharn. Anne Lorne Gillies, the Gaelic singer, is a well-known bearer of this name.

Lyle (*m.*)
A surname (French *l'île*, meaning 'the island') occasionally adopted as a first name.

Machar (*m.*)
From the Gaelic for a plainsman, or 'man of the machair'. St Machar was a follower of Columba who took the Christian message to Aberdeen, of which he is the patron saint.

Magnus (*m.*)

Gaelic **Manas**

The Latin word for 'great', which became popular in Europe after the reign of Carolus Magnus, better known as the Emperor Charlemagne. St Olaf of Norway christened one of his sons after the great emperor, and the name then became widespread in Scandinavia. It travelled thence into Shetland and Orkney, where St Magnus built the cathedral at Kirkwall (where he is buried). Magnus Magnusson, the broadcaster, has perhaps popularized the name in the 1970s and 1980s.

Mairi (*f.*)

This is the Gaelic for **Mary**, with the stress on the first syllable. It is sometimes spelled Mhairi (và'ree), which is the vocative form of the name. Common diminutives are Màili (Molly) and Moire (**Moira**).

Malcolm (*m.*)

Gaelic **MaolCholuim**

From Gaelic for 'tonsured servant of St Columba'. Four early Scots kings bore this name, most famously Malcolm III, called Canmore (or 'big head') (*c.*1031–93), husband of Queen Margaret. Long popular in Scotland, the name has now spread throughout the English-speaking world (Malcolm Sargent, orchestral conductor; Malcolm Muggeridge, broadcaster; Malcolm Fraser, Australian Prime Minister 1975–83). (See also **Calum**.)

Margaret (*f.*)

Gaelic **Mairead**

From Latin *margareta*, derived from the Greek word for 'a pearl'. The name was popular in Eastern Europe in the Middle Ages through the influence of the third-century martyr St Margaret of Antioch. St Margaret (1046–93), wife of King Malcolm III of Scotland, brought the name from Hungary, where she was born. Common diminutives and pet forms are Maisie, Maggie, Peggy, Margo and Rita.

Marie (*f.*)

The French form of **Mary**, with the stress on the second syllable, perhaps popular in Scotland as a result of the Auld Alliance and the influence of Mary Queen of Scots. Some Scottish parents still prefer this form to Mary.

Marion (*f.*)
A diminutive of Mary, sometimes associated with Gaelic **Mòrag**.

Marjorie, **Margery** (*f.*)
Gaelic **Marsaili**
Marjorie is from French *marguerite*, the flower. It became popular in Scotland in the 14th century after King Robert the Bruce gave the name to his daughter. It was Marjorie Bruce who married Walter the High Steward and founded the royal house of **Stewart**. The Gaelic name is from Latin Marcella, the female version of Marcus (from Mars, Roman god of war).

Mary (*f.*)
Gaelic **Mairi**
Mary probably represents the Greek version of Miriam, the Hebrew name for 'a wished-for child'. As the name for the mother of Jesus Christ, Mary was long felt to be too sacred for general use. It has been popular since the 12th century, but is now in decline with the trend away from conservative names. (See also **Mairi**, **Marie**.)

Matthew (*m.*)
Gaelic **Mata**
The name of one of the twelve apostles, from the Hebrew for 'gift of God', and long a popular name in Scotland. Matt and Mattie are diminutive forms.

Maxwell (*m.*)
A Scottish placename (Maccus – well, a reach of the Tweed near Kelso) which yielded the clan name, now also used as a forename.

Melville (*m.*)
A Norman-French placename which became a Scottish surname. Now also occasionally found as a forename.

Merrick (*m.*)
The name of a mountain in Kirkcudbrightshire, the highest in the Southern Uplands (2766 ft/843 m), in occasional use as a forename.

Michael (*m.*)
Gaelic **Micheal**
From Hebrew, meaning 'who is like God?' The apostle Michael is regarded as the patron saint of soldiers, horsemen and seafarers. The name was popular in Scotland during the Middle Ages, but dropped out of currency by the 19th century. Mike and Mick are diminutives.

Moira (*f.*)
Gaelic **Moire**
This was the Gaelic version of **Mairi** previously restricted in use to the mother of Jesus Christ, now quite widespread in Scotland and Ireland. The singer Moira Anderson may have encouraged the spread of the name.

Mòrag (*f.*)
A diminutive of Gaelic *mor*, 'great', sometimes associated with **Marion**. In the days when Jacobites furtively drank the health of the outlawed Bonnie Prince Charlie in the 18th century, it was far too risky to refer to him by name: they merely passed their winecups over the water (-jug) and murmured a toast to 'Mòrag'.

Morna (*f.*)
From Gaelic *muirne*, 'beloved'. Popular in Scotland and Ireland.

Morven, Morvern (*f.*)
A forename from Scottish placenames (Morven in Caithness being *mor bheinn*, 'big ben'; Morvern in Argyll being *mor bhearna*, 'big pass'). Sometimes linked with another forename, eg Morven-Ann.

Muir (*m.*)
The Scots word for a heath or moor became a surname for people living near one. It was one of the 100 commonest Scots surnames in 1976, according to the Registrar General, and is also in occasional use as a forename.

Mungo (*m.*)
Gaelic **Mungan**
From Welsh Gaelic Munghu, meaning 'amiable' or 'beloved'. It was the pet name of St Kentigern, sixth-

century bishop and patron saint of Glasgow. The most famous modern bearer of the name was Mungo Park (1771–1806) who charted the course of the river Niger in West Africa. Mungo Jerry was a pop musician of the 1960s.

Murdo (m.)
Gaelic **Murchadh/Muireach**
The two Gaelic names are rendered as Murdo, or occasionally Murdoch, in English. Muireach was the name of a ninth-century saint, and meant 'lord'. Murchadh was formerly a common name in **MacKenzie** country, and meant 'sea warrior'. The name has been recorded as Murder by English registrars unfamiliar with Scots nomenclature.

Muriel (f.)
Gaelic **Muireall**
The Gaelic name is from *muir* ('sea') and *geal* ('bright'), and has long been popular in Ireland and in steady use in Scotland. Muriel Spark (1918–), author of *The Prime of Miss Jean Brodie* (1961), and Muriel Gray, TV personality, are contemporary bearers of the name.

Murray, Moray (m.)
Gaelic **Moireach**
The province of Moray in north-east Scotland takes its name from Celtic for 'a seaboard settlement'. William of Moray was the founder of the clan in the 12th century, and the name later took the commoner Murray spelling and spread widely. It is now also in occasional use as a forename. Moray McLaren was a well-known broadcaster and raconteur of the 1950s.

Neil (m.)
Gaelic **Niall**
From the Celtic word for a champion. The name also went into Norse as Njal, who was one of the heroes of the Icelandic sagas. Clan **MacNeil** derives from this name. The Gaelic diminutive of Niall is Nilidh (nee'ly). The English name is sometimes spelled Neal and is related to Nigel.

Nelly (*f.*)
Gaelic **Neillidh**
The Gaelic name is a diminutive of Eibhlin while the English name is a pet form of Ellen or **Helen**.

Nessie (*f.*)
A diminutive of **Agnes** which was popular in Scotland in the late 19th and early 20th century. The shy and elusive megastar which bears this name is, of course, the Loch Ness Monster.

Nicol (*m.*)
Gaelic **Niocal**
A Scottish diminutive of Nicolas, from Greek meaning 'victory of the people'. The cult of St Nicolas made it a popular medieval name which in due course gave surnames **Nicol**, **MacNicol** and **Nicolson**. The Glasgow magistrate Bailie Nicol Jarvie was a character in Scott's novel *Rob Roy* (1817). Nicola is a female form, recently popular in Scotland.

Norman (*m.*)
Gaelic **Tormod**
In Old English the name means 'north man' while the Gaelic name is from Norse meaning 'Thor's wrath' (Thor was the Norse god of war). The diminutive is Norrie (Noraidh), and the female form is Norma.

Olaf (*m.*)
Gaelic **Olghar**
An Old Norse name, meaning 'ancestor-relic', still widely used in Orkney and Shetland.

Oscar (*m.*)
From Old Norse for a 'divine spear'. In the Celtic sagas, Oscar was the son of Ossian (Oisin) and grandson of **Fingal** (Fionn mac Cumhail). The name fell from favour after the Oscar Wilde scandal but may be making a recovery. Oscar Marzaroli was a famous Scottish photographer of the 1970s and 1980s.

Patrick (*m.*)
Gaelic **Pàdraig**
From Latin *patricius*, a nobleman or patrician. A popular Christian name in Scotland in the Middle Ages, where the Celtic Church had many followers of

St Patrick. The surname **Paterson** (Patrick's son) is from this source. Patrick Sellar, the wicked factor of the inglorious Dukes of Sutherland in the early 19th century, may have dented the name's popularity in the Highlands for a period. Diminutive versions of the name are Pat and Paddy in English, Pàraig and Para in Gaelic. Para has been popularized by the fictional Clyde puffer-captain Para Handy. The female form Patricia has been popular since the 19th century.

Paul (*m.*)
Gaelic **Pol**

From Latin *paulus*, meaning 'small', steadily used in Scotland since the Middle Ages. Surnames such as Polson, **MacPhail** and Paulin are from this source. Paul Jones was a Scottish sea captain from Kirkcudbright who served in the American navy during the War of Independence. A popular dance is named after him. Female versions of the name are Pauline and Paula.

Peggy (*f.*)
Gaelic **Peigi**

Diminutive versions of **Margaret**/Mairead which have acquired popularity in their own right. Burns wrote poems about several Peggies – including 'Bonny Peggy Alison' and 'Montgomerie's Peggy'.

Peter (*m.*)
Gaelic **Peadar**

From Greek *petros*, 'a rock'. Peter was the chief apostle of Jesus Christ and first bishop of Rome, and became the favourite saint of the medieval Church. In steady use in Scotland from early times, the name enjoyed a strong revival after 1904 with the success of J. M. Barrie's *Peter Pan*. The town of Peterhead is named after the nearby promontory of St Peter, which had an ancient church on it dedicated to the saint.

Quintin, Quentin (*m.*)

From Latin *quintus*, fifth, in use occasionally as a forename for a fifth child. The name had a following in Dumfriesshire, where St Quentin was patron saint of Kirkmahoe. Scott's romance *Quentin Durward* (1823) may have revived interest in the name.

Ramsay (*m.*)
A Scottish surname and occasional forename from an English placename in Huntingdonshire. Ramsay MacDonald (1866–1937), Britain's first Labour Prime Minister, was a prominent holder of this forename.

Ranald, Ronald (*m.*)
Gaelic **Raghnall**
Derived from Norse Rognvaldr, meaning 'counsel rule'. St Rognvald (died 1185) was an Earl of Orkney and nephew of St Magnus, and was active in the establishment of Kirkwall cathedral. Ranald remains an exclusively Scottish name, but Ronald has become popular throughout the English-speaking world. Ronald Reagan, US President (1982–90), is a prominent bearer of the name. Common diminutives are Ron, Ronnie and Gaelic Ronaidh.

Randal, Rendel (*m.*)
Diminutive versions of Randolph in use in Scotland. Rendall is also an Orkney surname and may be an influence.

Richard (*m.*)
Gaelic **Ruiseart**
From Old German, meaning 'firm government', in use in Scotland from an early date. Many surnames including Dick, Dickie, **Dickson**, Dickinson, Richardson and **Ritchie** derive from this forename and its diminutives. The surname Ritchie has now gone full circle, as it were, and is now once again found as a forename.

Ringan (*m.*)
Gaelic **Truinnean**
A common forename in the 16th century and later, Ringan was a vernacular Scots version of **Ninian**. *Ringan Gilhaize* (1823) was John Galt's novel about the Covenanters.

Rob (*m.*)
Gaelic diminutive of **Robert**, used by Rob Ruadh Mac Griogair. (Rob Roy MacGregor, 1671–1734; Ruadh means 'red-haired'.)

Robert (m.)
Gaelic **Raibeart**

From the Old German for 'fame bright', immensely popular in Scotland after the triumphs of King Robert the Bruce, one of the nation's heroes. Robert Burns (1759–96), the poet, also popularized the name. Many surnames derive from the early use of this forename, including **Robertson**, Robson, **MacRobb**, MacRobert, MacRobbie. Obsolete diminutives Hob and Dob gave Hobson, Dobson, Dobbinson and **Dobbie**. Current diminutives include Rab, Rabbie, Bob, **Robin** and Gaelic **Rob** and Robaidh.

Robin (m.)
Gaelic **Roban**

French and Gaelic diminutives of **Robert**, popularized by Burns in songs such as 'Rantin, rovin Robin'.

Roderick (m.)
From the Old German for 'fame rule'. A popular family forename among the MacNeils and generally in wide use throughout Scotland in the 19th century. The diminutive Roddy is associated with Gaelic Rodaidh (pronounced 'ro'dy'), which is in fact a diminutive of Ruairidh. Rod is also in use, for example by Rod Stewart, a pop star of the 1980s.

Rona, Rhona (f.)
Probably from the names of two Scottish islands off the west coast. (Other examples of this trend are **Ailsa** and **Iona**.) There may also be an echo of **Rowena** in the name. Gaelic Rìona (pronounced 'ree'nu') is really a diminutive of **Catrìona** and is usually anglicized as Rena.

Rònan (m.)
A Gaelic name, a diminutive of *ron*, a seal or sea creature. There was a St Ronan in the seventh century who spent time as a hermit on Lewis and on **Rona**. St Ronan's Well at Innerleithen in the Borders gave a title to a novel by Sir Walter Scott (1824).

Rory (*m.*)
Gaelic **Ruairidh**
From Gaelic *ruadh*, meaning 'red-haired'. Popular among Irish and Scots Gaels from the 12th century. In the 19th century there was some confusion with Roderick, which sounds similar, and which was adopted as a more English substitute.

Ronald see **Ranald**.

Rose (*f.*)
Gaelic **Ròs**
One of the most popular of the flower names, fashionable from the 19th century. Many variants have been adopted, including Rosalind (probably from German), Roslin or Rosslyn (perhaps from the place in Midlothian), Rosaleen or Rosaline (perhaps from Shakespeare). There has also been a tendency to use Rose as a second forename, as in Mary Rose or Margaret Rose. There is also clan **Rose**, with lands in Nairn and a shared ancestry with the **Ross** clan, which may have encouraged the forename.

Rosemary (*f.*)
A very popular forename in Scotland in the 1950s, from the plant name deriving from Latin *ros* ('dew') and *marinus* ('of the sea'). The name is also, of course, a simple combination of **Rose** and **Mary**.

Ross (*m.*)
Gaelic **Ros**
A clan name which was given to a Highland county (Ross and Cromarty) and which has more recently found favour as a forename in Scotland, Canada and Australia. The geographical name may also be derived from Gaelic *ros*, a promontory or headland, as in local placenames Fortrose and Rosemarkie.

Rowena (*f.*)
From Welsh *rhonwen*, 'slender fair'. Sir Walter Scott popularized the name by giving it to the heroine of *Ivanhoe* (1819). Rowena Farre is a modern author, whose *Seal Morning* (1970) is set in the north-west Highlands.

Roy (*m.*)

An anglicized version of *ruadh*, Gaelic for 'red-haired'. Rob Roy MacGregor (1671–1734) was really 'red-haired' Rob MacGregor, but Sir Walter Scott's novel *Rob Roy* (1817) popularized Roy in its own right. (The name did not derive from *roi*, the French word for 'king'.)

Russell (*m.*)

A first name from a common Scottish surname. The surname derives from French *roux*, 'red-haired'. Interestingly, the feminine of *roux* is *rousse*, from which clan names **Ross** and **Rose** may derive. In the mists of time therefore, **Rose** and Russell could have been sister and brother!

Samuel (*m.*)

From the Hebrew 'heard by God'. A biblical name popular in Scotland from the Reformation to the early 20th century, but now infrequent. Sam and Sammy were popular diminutives, and Uel was also known. Samuel was sometimes used as an English substitute for **Sorley** or Gaelic Somhairle.

Sandy (*m.*)
Gaelic **Sandaidh**

A diminutive of **Alexander**. It is sometimes claimed that Sandy is the preferred diminutive in the west of Scotland while Alec or Alex is preferred in the east. Sandy also gave the nickname Sawney, most notably to the celebrated criminal Sawney Bean. Outside Scotland, the name has been used for females, with the spelling Sandie (notably by Sandie Shaw, a pop star of the 1960s).

Sarah (*f.*)
Gaelic **Sàra**

From the Hebrew for queen or princess, a popular biblical name in Scotland after the Reformation. In the Old Testament, Sarah was the wife of the prophet Abraham. Sally is a popular diminutive version, and Sadie is also found occasionally.

Scott (*m.*)
Gaelic **Scotaidh**

From the racial name of the Scoti, or Scotti, the original Scots tribe which came from Ireland and settled in Dalriada (Argyll) in the sixth century. The surname – and clan name – became very widespread (the 12th most-frequent Scottish surname in 1976). In the 13th century the name was borne by Michael Scot, the scientist and 'Wizard' of Balwearie; and by John Duns Scotus, the medieval scholar and theologian. Sir Walter Scott more recently added lustre to the name. The vogue of the forename seems to have started in the USA with people like the writer Scott Fitzgerald and the jazz musician Scott Joplin. It has been very popular in Scotland since the 1970s.

Seàn (*m.*)
The Irish Gaelic form of Scots Gaelic Iain, or English **John**, sometimes anglicized as Shane or Shaun. The use of the name has spread in Scotland from the 1970s probably following the fame of Sean Connery, the Scottish actor best known for his James Bond films.

Senga (*f.*)
The name **Agnes** spelt backwards is only found in Scotland. It has been in use since the late 19th century.

Seònaid (*f.*)
A common Gaelic name cognate with **Janet** and **Janice**. It derives from Hebrew Johanan, 'grace of God', and has been anglicized as **Jane**, **Jean** or **Joan**. Diminutives include Seona (anglicized as **Shona**), Seonag and Seas (anglicized as Jess).

Seònaidh (*m.*)
A common Gaelic diminutive of Iain, anglicized as Johnny.

Seumas (*m.*)
A common Gaelic name deriving from Hebrew Jacob. It is cognate with **James** in English, and also gives the name **Hamish** from its vocative form 'a Sheumais'.

Sheena (*f.*)
Gaelic **Sìne**
Sheena probably entered English via Gaelic Sìne, which is a derivative of Hebrew Johanan, 'grace of God'. Sheona has become a popular spelling, perhaps influenced by Gaelic **Seònaid**.

Sheila (f.)
Gaelic **Sìle/Sìlis**

Derived from Latin Cecilia, who was a Roman martyr (died 230) and is the patron saint of church music and musicians. Another cognate of the name is Celia. Variant spellings of Sheila include Sheelagh, Shelagh and Shiela.

Shona (f.)
Gaelic **Seònaid**

This is the common phonetic spelling of Gaelic **Seònaid**. Other spellings are Shonag and Sheona.

Sinclair (m.)
From a Norman placename (Saint-Claire-sur-Elle) which became a common Scottish surname and clan name, and was the family name of the Earls of Orkney and Caithness. The forename has gained wide currency in the 20th century (Sinclair Lewis, US novelist 1885–1951).

Sorley (m.)
Gaelic **Somhairle**

The Gaelic name derives from Old Norse *sumar* ('summer'), *lithi* ('sailor, or wanderer'), and meant a Viking. It gave the old name of Somerled, taken by several Lords of the Isles. The most famous recent bearer of the name is the Gaelic poet Sorley MacLean (Somhairle Mac-Gill-Ean, born 1911), who in 1990 won the Queen's Gold Medal for Poetry.

Steven, Stephen (m.)
Gaelic **Steafan**

From Greek *stephanos*, a laurel garland or crown. Steven was the first Christian martyr and the name has been popular in all European languages. Steve and Stevie are popular diminutives. An early pronunciation of the name was Steen, with diminutive Steenie, giving surnames Steen and Stein. Steenie Steenson, properly Steven Stevenson, was a comic character in Scott's novel *Redgauntlet* (1824).

Stirling (m.)
From the placename (etymology obscure) came the surname, and later the occasional forename. Stirling Moss, the racing driver, is a popular bearer of the name.

Struan (*m.*)
From the placename in Perthshire (etymology uncertain) comes this occasional forename.

Stuart, Stewart (*m.*)
Gaelic **Stiubhart**
The surname of the royal house of Scotland from 1371 till 1714, from Old English *sti weard*, meaning 'a steward'. The spelling Stuart was a French form adopted by Mary Queen of Scots in the 16th century, and is now the more popular spelling for the Christian name.

Sueno, Sweeny (*m.*)
Gaelic **Suibhne**
Perhaps linked to Sweyn, the name of three kings of Denmark in the 11th and 12th century. The Gaelic name was in use by a lord of Galloway (died 1034) and is echoed in the surnames MacSween and **MacQueen** and in Loch Sween and Castle Sween (Argyll). Sueno's Stone, in Moray, is one of the most remarkable of standing stones intricately inscribed in the Pictish tradition, probably to commemorate some forgotten battle between the Vikings and the Picts. Sueno is thought to have been the name of the sculptor.

Teresa, Theresa (*f.*)
The name is probably of Greek origin, becoming popular in Spain by the Middle Ages. St Teresa of Avila (1515–82) and St Teresa of Lisieux (1873–97) popularized the name among Catholics throughout Europe. Popular modern diminutives of the name include Terry, Tessa and Tracey.

Thelma (*f.*)
A name invented in the 19th century by the novelist Marie Corelli which became popular in Scotland and England, and later in North America. The Greek word *thelma* means 'will' and may have lent the name etymological respectability. (Compare **Fiona**.)

Thomas (*m.*)
Gaelic **Tòmas**
As the name of one of the 12 apostles, Thomas has long been popular in most European languages.

Tammas (Gaelic Tàmhas) is the popular Scots version of the name. Tom and Tommy are popular diminutives. Surnames deriving from this Christian name include **Thom**, Thomas, **Thomson**, MacThomas, MacComish, MacCombie and **MacTavish**. An early Scottish bearer of the name was the poet and seer Thomas the Rhymer, or Thomas Rymour of Erceldoune (c.1220–97). He lived at Erceldoune (now Earlston) in Berwickshire and is credited with predicting the death of King Alexander III and the battle of Bannockburn. His prophetic powers earned him the name of 'True Thomas'.

Timothy (*m.*)
From the Greek word for honour. The name was used as a substitute for Gaelic Tadg, a poet or philosopher.

Tormod (*m.*)
A common Gaelic name deriving from the Norse Thormothr, meaning 'Thor's wrath'. Thor was the Norse god of war. (See **Norman**, with which the name is popularly associated.)

Torquil (*m.*)
Gaelic **Torcall**
From the Norse name Thorketill ('Thor's kettle, or holy vessel'), Thor being the Norse god of war. The forename has been specially popular in the **MacLeod** clan.

Turval (*m.*)
A Shetland name deriving from Norse Thorvald, meaning 'Thor the ruler'.

Uilleag (*f.*) see **Wilma**.

Uilleam (*m.*) see **William**.

Uisdean (*m.*)
A Gaelic forename of uncertain meaning sometimes associated with **Hugh**.

Una (*f.*)
A common Christian name in Irish and Scots Gaelic, sometimes anglicized as Oonagh or Oona. The name may be from Irish *uan*, a lamb.

Victoria (f.)

The Latin word for victory. The name was only occasionally used in Scotland or England before the reign of Queen Victoria (1837–1901), since when it has been much in vogue. Vicky is a popular diminutive (with variant spellings Vikki, Vicki and Vickie.)

Vincent (m.)

From Latin *vinxit*, 'he conquered'. St Vincent de Paul (c.1580–1660) founded the Sisterhood of Charity and the Congregation of Mission Priests popularized the name among Catholic families. Admiral Nelson's naval victory at Cape St Vincent (1797) widened this appeal – St Vincent Street in Glasgow being named after this battle.

Violet (f.)

One of the many flower names popular in Scotland, where it has been in use since the 16th century. The name probably originated in France, where in the early 19th century it became the badge of supporters of the exiled Napoleon.

Wallace (m.)

Gaelic **Uallas**

From the surname of Scotland's great patriot and resistance fighter (c.1274–1305). The use of the forename has now spread beyond Scotland – see for example Wallis Simpson (1896–1987), the American-born Duchess of Windsor, and Wallace Stevens (1879–1955), the American poet.

Walter (m.)

Gaelic **Bhaltair**

From an Old German name Waldhar, meaning 'rule people'. It was Walter the High Steward (died 1177) whose descendants formed the Scottish royal house of Stewart. Sir Walter Scott (1771–1832) greatly boosted the name's popularity. Wat and Wattie are popular diminutives. Surnames **Watt**, Wattie and **Watson** derive from early use of these forenames in Scotland.

Wendy (f.)

Like **Fiona**, this name is a literary invention, first used by J. M. Barrie in the story of *Peter Pan* (1904). Apparently Barrie got the name from a child friend of his, Margaret Henley, who gave Barrie the pet name 'Friendy-Wendy'. Wendy Wood was a colourful 20th-century Scottish nationalist political figure.

William (m.)

Gaelic **Uilleam**

From the Old German name Wilihelm, meaning 'willpower-helmet'. The name became popular in Scotland after King William the Lyon (1143–1214) and Sir William Wallace (*c.*1274–1305), the great patriot. Diminutives include Willie (Gaelic Uillidh) – immortalized in 'Wee Willie Winkie' – and Bill or Billy. King William of Orange (1650–1702) is popularly referred to as King Billy. Derived surnames include **MacWilliam**, **Williamson** and **Wilson**.

Wilma (f.)

Gaelic **Uilleag**

Feminine versions of **William**/Uilleam. Wilma was not often found outside Scotland before the appearance of Wilma (Fred Flintstone's wife) in the American TV series, *The Flintstones*.

Wilson (m.)

A Scottish surname which evolved through early use of the forenames **William** and Will (Will's son). Wilson is now occasionally found as a forename, which is an example of the etymological wheel turning full circle.

Yvonne (f.)

A French feminine diminutive of the male Christian name Yves. The male name never caught on in Britain, though it gave the placename St Ives in Cornwall, and was taken by a Robert Louis Stevenson hero in the novel *St Ives* (1897). Yvonne was very popular in Scotland around the mid-20th century.

SURNAMES

Abercrombie, Abercromby
From a barony in Fife, now called St Monans. William de Abercromby of Fife did homage in 1296. Sir Patrick Abercrombie (1877–1957) was a celebrated architect and town planner.

Abernethy
From the placename in Strathearn, Perthshire. The first of the name appear to have been lay abbots of the monastery of Abernethy in the 12th century. The family had the (comparatively rare) privilege of sanctuary before the Reformation.

Adair
A Galloway name from about the 14th century, probably derived from the forename Edgar.

Adam
From the popular forename, recorded from the 12th century. Related surnames are Adie (diminutive of Adam), Adams, Adamson and **MacAdam**. The classical architect Robert Adam (1728–92) was an eminent holder of the name.

Affleck
From two villages: Affleck in Angus, and Auchinleck in Ayrshire. Recorded from the 13th century.

Agnew
From the Norman-French Baronie d'Agneaux (Vire). They may originally have been shepherds, because *agneau* means 'a lamb'. The family were appointed hereditary sheriffs of Galloway in 1363 by King David II, and later became a prominent landowning family there.

Aiken, Aitken, Atkin, Atkins

Double diminutives of **Adam** (Adie + kin), early found as forenames ('Aiken Drum'). In Orkney, Aiken is said to have replaced Haakon and Hakonson. Recorded from the 14th century.

Aikenhead

From lands in Lanarkshire, probably derived from an early owner called **Aiken**. Recorded as a surname from the 14th century.

Aitchison, Acheson, Atkinson

All these names derive from diminutives of **Adam**; Atty for the first two giving Atty's son, Adkin for the last giving Adkin's son. Recorded from the 14th century.

Alexander

From the quickly popular forename introduced into Scotland by Queen Margaret (died 1093) from the Hungarian court where she was raised. The surname is recorded from *c.*1300.

Alison, Allison, Ellison

From 'son of Ellis, or Elias', recorded from the 13th century. The female forename Alison began to appear in the 15th century, perhaps influenced by **Alice**.

Allan, Allen

From Old Gaelic Ailin (*ail*, 'a rock'), which also gives the name Alwyn; and from *alainn* ('beautiful'), as in Allan Water and Bridge of Allan, near Stirling. Norman–French Alain/Alan (from Germanic Alemannus, the German racial name) was also influential in circulating this surname recorded from the 13th century. (See also **MacAllan**.)

Allardyce

From lands by the Bervie Water in Kincardineshire. Recorded from the 13th century.

Anderson

From 'son of **Andrew**', a surname widespread in Scotland and recorded from the 13th century. Sir

John Anderson (1882–1958) was the war-time Home Secretary whose name is commemorated by the Anderson air-raid shelter.

Annan, Annand

From the town and river in Dumfriesshire, recorded as a surname from the 13th century. J. K. Annand (born 1908) is a humorous Scots poet.

Arbuckle

From the placename in Lanarkshire, recorded from the 15th century.

Arbuthnot, Arbuthnott

From lands in Kincardineshire. Hugh de Aberbothenoth acquired an estate here, c.1200. John Arbuthnot (1667–1735) was a physician, poet and wit, and a friend of Swift and Pope.

Armour

From the trade of armourer, a maker of armour. The name is recorded from the 13th century. Jean Armour (1767–1834) was the wife of the poet Robert Burns.

Armstrong

The famous Border surname of a clan based in Liddesdale in Dumfriesshire. The original bearer of the name had a strong arm, as had his Norman counterpart (*fort en bras* giving the surname Fortinbras), and it is recorded in Scotland from the 14th century. The reiver Johnnie Armstrong of Gilnockie was summarily executed by James V in 1529, an episode which has been immortalized in ballad and legend. The American Neil Armstrong (born 1930) was the first man on the moon.

Arneil

From the placename Ardneill, and Ardneill Bay, at West Kilbride in Ayrshire. Recorded from the 17th century.

Arnott, Arnot

From lands near Portmoak, in Kinross. Recorded from the 13th century.

Arrol

From Errol in Perthshire. Recorded from the 16th century. Sir William Arrol (1839–1913) was a famous civil engineer and contractor for the Forth Bridge and the (second) Tay Bridge.

Auchinloss, Auchincloss

From lands near Kilmarnock, in Ayrshire. Recorded from the 15th century.

Auchterlonie, Ochterlonie

From lands near Forfar, in Angus. Walter de Ochterlovenig rendered homage in 1296. From 1860 to 1930 Willie Auchterlonie and his son Laurie were golf professionals and club makers at the Royal and Ancient Golf Club, St Andrews, where Willie also won the 1893 Open.

Auld

A surname meaning 'old' which, like Elder, probably originated with the purpose of distinguishing father from son when both bore the same Christian name. Recorded from the 13th century.

Baillie, Bailie, Bailey

Originally indicated the office of bailiff or bailie, derived from Norman–French *bailli*. Lady Grizel Baillie (1665–1746) and Joanna Baillie (1762–1851) are remembered for their songs.

Bain, Bane, Bayne

From Gaelic *ban*, meaning 'fair', recorded from the 15th century. Compare the surname **Bell**.

Baird

The name could have indicated the occupation of bard, or poet. Or it may be territorial, from lands near Lesmahagow in Lanarkshire. Recorded from the 14th century. John Logie Baird (1888–1946) was an inventor of television.

Balderston, Balderstone

From lands in West Lothian, the tun of Balder. William de Baudrestone of Linlithgow rendered homage in 1296.

Balfour
From the barony of Balfour, near Markinch in Fife. The surname spread through Fife from the 14th century and a branch settled in Orkney in the 18th century. A. J. Balfour (1848–1930) was a Conservative Prime Minister, and was responsible for the 1917 Balfour Declaration promising a national homeland in Palestine to Zionists.

Ballantyne, Ballantine
Probably from the lands of Bellenden in Roxburghshire, recorded from the 15th century. John Bellenden (died 1587) was the translator of Livy and of Boece's *History of Scotland* (1527) into Scots. (See also **Bannatyne**.)

Bannatyne
Perhaps from the placename on Bute, recorded from the 14th century. For a long time the name was interchangeable with **Ballantyne**. George Bannatyne (1545–1608) was an Edinburgh burgess and editor whose 'Bannatyne Manuscript' preserved much 15th- and 16th-century Scots poetry.

Bannerman
A name popularly believed, after Boece (died 1536), to originate in the occupation of royal standard-bearer, or king's banner-man. Recorded from the 14th century.

Barbour, Barber
From the occupation of barber (and surgeon, with which it was combined in the Middle Ages), recorded from the 14th century. John Barbour (*c*.1316–96) wrote the epic poem *The Brus* (1370s) and has been called 'the father of Scots poetry'.

Barclay
From the English placename Berkeley, in Gloucestershire. Walter de Berchelai was Chamberlain of Scotland in 1165. Colonel David Barclay (1610–86) served under Gustavus Adolphus of Sweden in the Thirty Years War, and acquired great wealth. The Russian general Barclay de Tolly (1761–1818) was of Scottish ancestry. Willie Barclay (1907–78) was a popular religious broadcaster and writer.

Barr

From placenames Barr and Barrhill in Ayrshire, and Barrhead in Renfrewshire. (In Gaelic *barr* means 'top' or 'head', so Barrhead is a tautology.) Atkin de Barr was an Ayr bailie in the 14th century. Archibald Barr (1855–1931) was a professor of engineering who with William Stroud founded the famous Glasgow firm of scientific instrument-makers: Barr and Stroud.

Barrie

From a placename in Angus, recorded from the 14th century. Sir J. M. Barrie (1860–1937) was a successful author, of *Peter Pan* (1904) and many other plays and novels.

Baxter

From the Old English word for a baker, recorded as a surname from the 13th century. The nucleus of the Edinburgh Baxters was the village of Dean and its flour-mills along the Water of Leith.

Beaton

Originally a person from Bethune, in northern France. Recorded from the 12th century. Beaton and Gaelic **Macbeth** became confused in parts of the Hebrides in the 16th century. The hereditary physicians to the **MacLeans** of Duart on Mull were Beatons. Cardinal David Beaton (1494–1546) was assassinated at St Andrews after his persecution of the Protestant reformers. Mary Beaton is remembered in song as one of the four Marys of Mary Queen of Scots.

Beattie, Beatty

A Border surname, from Bate or Batie, diminutive forms of Bartholomew. Recorded from the 14th century. James Beattie (1735–1803) was known for his long poem *The Minstrel*.

Begg

From the Gaelic word for 'small', *beag*. The Beggs were Earls of Levenax, or Lennox, 1225–1300.

Bell

Probably from two main sources: firstly Old French *Le bel*, the handsome man, as in King Philippe Le Bel (1268–1314). The other source suggests the bearer's occupation of bell-ringer, or residence beside the town bell. Recorded from the 13th century. Alexander Graham Bell (1847–1922) was the Scots-born inventor of the telephone.

Bennet, Bennett

From Benedict, via French Benoît. A common surname in Roxburgh and Edinburgh by the 16th century. James Gordon Bennett (1795–1872) was the Scots-born founder of the *New York Herald* (1835).

Bisset, Bissett

English courtiers of King William the Lyon brought this name to Scotland in the 12th century. A 13th-century bloodfeud between Bissets, Lords of Aboyne and the Earls of Atholl is well documented.

Black

Like **Gray**, **Brown** and **White**, this surname is from an early nickname. In early charters, Black was rendered in Latin as *Niger*. Gaelic for black is *dubh*, giving surnames Dow and **Duff**. Recorded from the 13th century. Adam Black (1784–1874) was twice Lord Provost of Edinburgh and founded the publishing firm of A. and C. Black.

Blackadder

From the Blackadder water and district of Berwickshire. Recorded from the 15th century. Robert Blackadder was Bishop of Glasgow in the 15th century, and the cathedral has a Blackadder chapel.

Blackie

A diminutive of **Black**, recorded from the 16th century. John Blackie (1782–1874) established the Glasgow publishing business which still bears his name.

Blacklock

Originally a name from a nickname, someone with black locks (ie black hair). The name is most widespread in Dumfries and Galloway, and is recorded from the 15th century. Dr Thomas Blacklock of Annan (1721–91) was a blind minister and poet, and also a friend of Burns.

Blair

A surname from a geographical location. Gaelic *blar* means 'a plain', and yielded many placenames (Blair Atholl, Blairgowrie, Blairmore, Blairlogie, etc). So Alexander de Blare, witness to a charter by Fergus, Earl of Buchan around 1214, was Alexander 'of the plain'. Eric Blair (1903–50), better known by his pseudonym George Orwell, was the author of *Animal Farm* (1945), *Nineteen Eighty-Four* (1949) and other modern classics.

Bone

Perhaps from French *le bon* ('the good'), or even possibly from the Norman–French surname De Bohun. Sir Henry de Bohun was the English knight who tried to kill King Robert the Bruce on the eve of the battle of Bannockburn (1314). Sir Muirhead Bone (1876–1953) was a well-known Glasgow artist.

Borthwick

From placenames in Midlothian and Roxburgh. Recorded from the 14th century.

Bowie

A nickname from Gaelic *buidhe*, 'yellow or fair-haired'. Recorded from the 15th century.

Bowman

Probably signified a small farmer or cattle herdsman (*bow* meaning cattle in Scots), rather than an archer. Recorded from the 14th century.

Boyd

Probably from the Gaelic name for Bute, Bod. Recorded in Ayrshire from the 13th century. Zachary Boyd (*c*.1585–1653) was a famous divine and author of *Zion's Flowers* (1644), popularly known as 'Boyd's Bible'. John Boyd Orr (1880–1971) was a Scots biologist, and winner of the Nobel Peace Prize in 1949.

Bremner, Brebner

Originally indicated people from Brabant, in the Low Countries. So Thomas the Brabanter became Thomas Brebener by the 16th century, thence Bremner by the 17th.

Brewster

From the occupation of brewer (compare **Baxter** and **Dempster**). Thomas le Breuester of Lanarkshire rendered homage in 1296. Sir David Brewster (1781–1868) was a Scots physicist and inventor of the kaleidoscope.

Brims

From two headlands called Brims Ness facing each other across the Pentland firth, in Caithness and on the Orkney island of Hoy. Recorded from the 17th century.

Brodie

A surname and clan name from the lands of Brodie in Nairnshire. Recorded from the 14th century. The clan's early records were unfortunately destroyed when Lord Lewis Gordon burnt Brodie Castle in 1645. The name represented the ultimate in respectability with Miss Jean Brodie, eponymous heroine of the Muriel Spark novel (1961); and was also notorious from the exploits of Deacon William Brodie, the Edinburgh councillor and burglar, executed in 1788.

Brown

A surname from a nickname, meaning brown-haired, widespread in England and Scotland and, as Lebrun, in France. There was also a Gaelic name Mac a'briuthainn ('a judge, or brehon') which was often anglicized as Brown. Brown is recorded from the 12th century, Mac a'briuthainn from the 14th. The 18th-century Gaelic poetess who rejoiced in the splendid name of Diorbhorgail Nic a'Briuthainn was translated into English as plain Dorothy Brown. George Douglas Brown (1869–1902) was the author of the powerful *The House with the Green Shutters* (1901).

Bruce

An illustrious Scots surname and clan name derived from the Norman village of Brus, now Brix, near Cherbourg. There was a Robert de Brus in the army of William the Conqueror in 1066. His son Robert, Le Meschin (the younger), was granted lands in Annandale by King David I, and 200 years later a descendant took the throne of Scotland and liberated the kingdom from the 'auld enemy', England. The royal

Bruce line died out in the 14th century but a branch of the family became Earls of Elgin and retain this title today. James Bruce (1730–94) was an explorer of Abyssinia and the Blue Nile. William Spiers Bruce (1867–1921) was a polar explorer and a zoologist.

Bryce

From the forename, after Bricius, a fifth-century Gaulish saint and bishop of Tours. It was a common Christian name in Scotland around 1200, and the surname entered the records about a hundred years later. David Bryce (1803–76) was the Edinburgh architect of Fettes College and the Royal Infirmary.

Bryson

From 'Bryce's son'. Duncan Briceson was an outlaw in the Mearns, 1392.

Buchan

From the district in Aberdeenshire. Recorded from about 1200. John Buchan (1875–1940) was the author of *Prester John* (1910), *The Thirty-Nine Steps* (1915), *Greenmantle* (1916) and other rattling good yarns, as well as finding time to be Governor-General of Canada and Chancellor of Edinburgh University.

Buchanan

From the district of Stirlingshire east of Loch Lomond. The name is from Gaelic *both* ('house, or bothy') and *chanain* ('of the canon'). George Buchanan (1506–82) was a famous Latin scholar and tutor to Mary Queen of Scots and her son James VI. James Buchanan (1791–1868) was the 15th US President and son of an immigrant Scots–Irish farmer.

Burns, Burn, Burnside

Bearers of these names originally lived near a burn. The poet Robert Burns (1759–96) was actually called Burness but decided to spell his name as Burns in 1786. The poet's father – and the name Burness – came from Kincardineshire.

Burrel, Burrell

From the village of Burrill in north Yorkshire. Recorded in Roxburghshire from the 12th century. Sir

William Burrell (1861–1958) was a Glasgow shipowner and art collector who gifted the Burrell Collection of works of art to the city.

Cadzow

From the lands of Cadyow, now Hamilton, in Lanarkshire. Adam de Cadiou rendered homage in 1296.

Caird

From Gaelic *ceard*, a craftsman. Most cairds worked in brass and other metals. In 1343 Robert Kerd made four horseshoes for King David II and also a jousting spear. Edward Caird (1835–1908) was an academic philosopher and his brother John (1820–98) was a famous preacher and principal of Glasgow University.

Cairncross

From lands in Angus, recorded from the 14th century.

Cairns

Perhaps from Gaelic *cairn* ('hill'); or from the parish of Cairns in Midlothian. Recorded from the 14th century in Lothian.

Cameron

From Gaelic *cam* ('crooked', 'hooked') and *sron* ('nose'), so the modern name is like **Campbell** in that it derives from a Gaelic nickname. Cambruns, Cambrons and Cambernons are recorded in the 13th century. The first documented clan chief is Donald Dhu in 1411. Donald Cameron of Locheil (1695–1748) was a key supporter of Bonnie Prince Charlie in 1745. Richard Cameron (1648–80) was a famous Covenanter, whose name is now carried by a lowland regiment of the British army, the Cameronians.

Campbell

From Gaelic *cam* ('crooked') and *beul* ('mouth'), rather an uncomplimentary nickname. (Compare **Cameron**.) The nickname origin of this name is corroborated by the fact that there is no Gaelic translation of Campbell, which is *Chlann O'Duibhne* in Gaelic. The traditional founder of the O'Duibhne was **Diarmid**, the legendary Fingalian warrior who killed the wild boar. Exactly when the O'Duibhnes became the Campbells is hard to say, but the earliest records of the surname Campbell date from the late 13th century. The Dukes of Argyll are the traditional clan chiefs. Thomas Campbell (1777–1844) was a poet, author of 'Lord Ullin's Daughter' and other popular pieces. The town of Campbeltown, in Kintyre, was called Kilkerran until the 18th century.

Cant
Originally Flemish cloth dealers, suppliers to the royal household in the 15th century. Richard Kant, the grandfather of the German philosopher Immanuel Kant (1724–1804), was a Scot.

Carmichael
From the lands of Carmichael in Lanarkshire; and possibly also from various places called Kirkmichael (Ayrshire, Perthshire). John Carmichael was a Scots-born bishop of Orleans (1429). Mary Carmichael was one of Mary Queen of Scots' 'Four Marys'.

Carnegie
From the lands of Carnegie in Angus. The surname is recorded from the 14th century. Andrew Carnegie (1837–1919), the Scottish-American industrialist and philanthropist, is the best-known bearer of this name.

Carruthers
From the lands of Carruthers, around Carruthers-town in Dumfriesshire. The name originally perhaps meant '**Roderick**'s fort'. The Carruthers family were stewards of Annandale in the 13th century under the **Bruce**s.

Carson, Corson
A Galloway surname of uncertain etymology, recorded from the 13th century. Thomas Acarsane was a royal minstrel in 1377.

Carswell, Cresswell
From lands in Renfrewshire, Lanarkshire and Roxburghshire. A Cressewelle and a Cresseville rendered homage in 1296. Catherine Carswell (1879–1946) was a novelist and author of a famous *Life of Robert Burns* (1930).

Cathcart

From lands beside the river Cart in Renfrewshire. *Cath* is Gaelic for 'a battle', so there may have been a long-forgotten battle by the side of the river Cart. (There was, of course, a better-documented, later battle here when in 1568 the Regent Moray defeated forces loyal to Mary Queen of Scots.) The name is recorded from the 13th century. There were three prominent military Cathcarts in the 19th century.

Cattanach

From Gaelic, meaning 'belonging to the clan Chattan'. The name is recorded from the 15th century and was widespread in parts of Aberdeenshire.

Chalmers, Chambers

Originally Chalmer and Chamber (from Old French *de la chambre*, and Latin *de camera*), from the profession of chamberlain or keeper of the royal chambers. The names seem to have evolved in the following sequence: de Camera and de la Chambre (12th and 13th centuries); Chaumir, Chamber, Chawemere (15th century); Chalmir (16th century), adding final -*s* in the 17th century. Thomas Chalmers (1780–1847) was a famous minister who established the Free Church of Scotland after the Disruption of 1843. William Chambers (1800–83) was a writer and publisher who, with his brother Robert (1802–71), founded the publishing imprint which carries their name today.

Chapman

A surname from the occupation of chapman, from Old English *ceapman*, a 'merchant'. Recorded from the 13th century. Walter Chepman and Andrew Myller established Scotland's first printing press at Edinburgh in 1507. The opening lines of Burns's *Tam o'Shanter* (1790) immortalize the race: 'When chapman billies leave the street . . .'

Charteris

Originally the name indicated people from Chartres, the cathedral town in northern France. Records from the 13th century list a variety of spellings: de Carnoto, de Cartres, and de Chartris.

Chisholm

A Border surname, from lands in Roxburghshire. A Chesholm and a Cheseholme rendered homage in 1296. Sir Robert de Cheseholme became constable of Urquhart Castle in Inverness-shire in 1359, and they then established themselves as a Highland clan, through marriage to local heiresses, by the 15th century. Alexander Chisholm (1792–1847) was a portrait painter.

Clark

Originally a clerk in holy orders, later a scholar or scribe. Latinized *clericus* in early records, the name had become common by the 14th century. When translated into Gaelic, it gave the surname **MacCleery** (Mac a'chleirich).

Clouston

An Orkney surname, from the place in Stenness parish. Sir Thomas Clouston was a 19th-century psychiatrist who practised in Edinburgh.

Cochrane

From lands near Paisley, recorded from the 13th century. They were Earls of Dundonald, and Thomas, the 10th Earl (1775–1860), was a British rear-admiral and was hailed as the 'liberator' of Chile and Peru.

Cockburn

From lands in Berwickshire, now Cockburnspath. Possibly from 'cuckoo' and 'burn'. Lord Cockburn (1779–1854) was a distinguished Scottish judge and writer. Pronounced 'Co-burn'.

Colquhoun

From lands in Dunbartonshire, where the name is recorded from the 13th century. The clan chief acquired by marriage the lands of Luss on Loch Lomond in the 14th century. One of the last inter-clan battles, at Glenfruin in 1603, was fought between Colquhouns and **MacGregors**. Pronounced 'Co-hoon'.

Coltrane

A Galloway surname of uncertain etymology, recorded from the 16th century. William Coltrane was a provost of Wigtown in the 1690s implicated in the drowning of covenanting martyrs. Robbie Coltrane is a TV entertainer of the 1980s and 1990s.

Cook, Cox

From the trade of cook, in Latin records *cocus*. The name was widespread in early documents from the 12th century.

Cooper, Coupar, Couper

From two sources: first, the trade of cooper or barrel-maker, and second, from the town of Cupar in Fife. The name is common in Fife records from the 13th century. (There is also the children's rhyme: 'There was a wee cooper who came from Fife . . .' which plays on the two sources of the name.)

Corrie

From lands in Dumfriesshire, recorded from the 13th century. Joe Corrie (1894–1968) wrote plays and poetry.

Corsar, Cousar

From the trade of horse dealer (Middle English *corser*), the names are first recorded in Berwickshire in the 14th century.

Coutts

From the district of Cults, west of Aberdeen. A William Coutts was provost of Montrose in the 16th century and his descendant Thomas Coutts (1735–1822) founded the London bank of Coutts and Company.

Cowan

Perhaps a corruption of **Colquhoun**. John Cowane of Stirling founded Cowane's Hospital in 1639.

Craig

From Gaelic *creag* ('hill' or 'crag'), the surname indicated people who lived near a crag. As a fairly craggy country, it is not surprising that the name is widespread in Scotland from the 13th century.

Cranston

The *tun* or lands of Cran: the name of a place in Midlothian. Cran, Crann or Crane were Old English forenames, and are also recorded as surnames around the Moray Firth. Elfric de Cranston was a charter witness in the 12th century. Kate Cranston commissioned Charles Rennie Mackintosh to design for her the famous Willow Tearooms in Sauchiehall Street, Glasgow in 1903.

Crawford, Craufurd

Ford of the crows: from the lands of Crawford in upper Lanarkshire. The mother of William Wallace (1274–1305) was a Crawford. The Earldom of Crawford is the oldest in Scotland still extant (created in 1398).

Crichton

From lands in Midlothian, spelled variously on early charters: Kreiton, Crectune, Crictannus, Kreytton and finally Crichton around 1250. J. M. Barrie's *The Admirable Crichton* (1902) is based on James Crichton (1560–82), son of the Scottish Lord Advocate. Pronounced 'Cry-ton'.

Crombie

From lands around Cromdale in Banffshire. The Gaelic *b* in the name is traditionally not pronounced. The name is recorded from the 15th century.

Cruikshank, Cruickshanks, Crookshanks

Two probable origins: a nickname, as might be guessed; but also perhaps a local name, from the river Cruik in Kincardineshire. The name is commonest in records of Aberdeen and Kincardine after 1400.

Cumming, Cummings, Cummine

The name originally indicated people who came from the town of Comines in northern France. By the 13th century the family of Comyn was extremely powerful in Scotland and controlled four earldoms. By 1309 Sir John Comyn ('the Red Comyn') was vying with Robert the Bruce for the Scottish throne. Bruce killed Comyn and broke the family's powers.

Cunningham, Cunninghame, Conyngham

From the name of the district of north Ayrshire. These lands were granted to a Norman knight whose descendant Richard de Cunningham was using the name of the land as a surname by 1210. There are Cunningham branches in France and Ireland.

Currie

Possibly an alternative spelling of **Corrie**. The place-name Currie in Midlothian does not appear to have given rise to a surname. Recorded from the 12th century.

Dalgleish, Dalgliesh, Dalglish

From lands in Ettrickdale, a surname recorded from 1407.

Dallas

From the old barony of Dallas in Morayshire. William de Dolays was sheriff of nearby Forres in 1292.

Dalrymple

From lands in south Ayrshire, in Gaelic 'the field of the curving stream' (*dail*='field', *chruimm*='curved', *puill*='stream'). The first charter reference to the name is in 1371. Kate Dalrymple is a catchy dance tune, named after a forgotten bearer of the name.

Dalyell, Dalziel

From the old barony of Dalziel in Lanarkshire (pronounced 'Dee-el'). Hugh de Dalyhel was sheriff of Lanark in 1288. General Thomas Dalyell (*c*.1599–1685) of the Binns in West Lothian was a professional soldier, who defeated the Covenanters at Rullion Green (1666). He was also a devoted royalist who never shaved his beard after the execution of King Charles I in 1649.

Dand, Dandie, Dandison

Surnames from the forename Dand or Dandie, diminutives of **Andrew** popular in the 16th century.

Danskin, Danskine

Originally the surname was used for people from Danzig (modern Gdansk) in the Baltic who settled in ports of the east of Scotland. Danzig was one of the Hanseatic trading towns. The name is recorded in Dundee from 1616 and in Crail from 1633.

Davidson, Davison

Originally meant 'the son of **David**'. The form Davison meant 'son of Davie', and of course the surname Davie is still in use. Another diminutive of

David was Daw, giving surnames Daw, Dawe, Dawes and Dawson. Early charters show Johannes filius Davidus or Adam fitz David giving way to Johan Davison around the middle of the 14th century. Randall Davidson (1848–1930) was a Scots-born archbishop of Canterbury.

Dean

From various Scottish placenames – in Aberdeen-shire and Ayrshire as well as the village of Dean in Edinburgh. The name may also have an ecclesiastical connection, and is recorded from the 15th century.

Dempster

The first Dempsters were law-givers (deemers), and there was a dempster or 'judex' attached to most courts to pronounce the 'doom'. A Haldan de Emester of Perthshire rendered homage in 1296. Thomas Dempster (c.1579–1625) wrote an erudite but notably unreliable history of the Church of Scotland.

Denholm

From places in Roxburghshire and Dumfriesshire, recorded from the 13th century.

Dewar

In Gaelic Deoir or Deoireach, from the Gaelic name for a pilgrim (*deoradh*). In the Middle Ages the *deoradh* was also the name for the custodian of a saint's bones or relics. Sir James Dewar (1842–1923) invented the vacuum flask and discovered cordite.

Dickson

Originally meant 'the son of Dick'. It was a Border surname and is recorded from the 14th century. Surnames with a similar etymology are Dick and Dickie.

Dinwiddie, Dinwoodie

From lands in Dumfriesshire. The surname is recorded in Annandale from the 13th century. Robert Dinwiddie (1693–1770) was governor of Virginia 1752–8, and proposed the annexation of Ohio.

Dobbie, Dobie

Surnames from pet forms of **Robert**, recorded from the 15th century. Surnames Dobieson and Dobson have similar etymologies.

Donald

In Gaelic *Domhnall* (early *Domnall*), a common personal name. By the 12th century the clan Donald had coalesced into the largest and most powerful of all the clans. Most Highland members of the clan rendered their surname as **MacDonald**, but the name is also recorded without the Mac from the 14th century.

Donaldson

An English version of **MacDonald**, meaning 'son of **Donald**', recorded from the 14th century. It is in the top hundred surnames in Scotland, according to the Registrar General (number 91 in 1990). James Donaldson (1751–1830) was a newspaper proprietor and philanthropist, the founder of Donaldson's Hospital in Edinburgh, a school for the deaf and dumb.

Dorward, Durward

Originally the surname was held by holders of the office of door-ward or warden at some of the great Scottish churches of the medieval period. Alan Durward was regent of Scotland during the minority of King Alexander III (1249). *Quentin Durward* (1823) is a novel by Sir Walter Scott.

Douglas

Originally the name of a stream and lands in upper Lanarkshire, from Gaelic *dubh glais* ('black water'). William de Duglas is the first recorded member of the family (1175) which later grew into a great clan vying with the power of the Scottish crown. The house of Douglas had four main strands in medieval times: the Black Douglases of Lanarkshire, whose Sir James Douglas – 'the good Sir James' – was Robert the Bruce's right-hand man in the Wars of Independence; the Douglas Earls of Morton in Dumfriesshire; the Red Douglas Earls of Angus; and the Drumlanrig-Queensberry Douglases. Gavin Douglas (*c*.1474–1522) was a poet and bishop of Dunkeld.

Drummond

From the barony in Stirlingshire around Drymen (a variant spelling). The first recorded Drummonds were witnesses to charters of the Earls of Levenax

(Lennox). Two Drummonds married into the royal house in the 14th century, and the chiefs of the clan became Earls of Perth. The Drummonds were strong Jacobites and lost ground after 1745. William Drummond of Hawthornden (1585–1649) was a poet and scientist.

Duff

From Gaelic *dubh* ('dark one'). Just as most of clan Domnall rendered their names as **MacDonald**, so most of clan Dubh gave theirs as **MacDuff**. But there were those of both names who did not take the Mac prefix. Duff is recorded as a surname from the 13th century, and Dufftown in Banffshire is named after this family. Alexander Duff (1806–78) was the first Scottish missionary to India.

Duguid

An Aberdeenshire surname of uncertain etymology, recorded from about 1300.

Duncan

From the Gaelic forename Donnchad. Records show Donchadus, Dunecanus and Wilhelmus filius Dunecan before 1200. The Highland clan Donnchaidh is rendered in English as **Robertson**. Admiral Duncan (1731–1804) was the victor of the sea battle of Camperdown (1797). Henry Duncan (1774–1846) was the minister of Ruthwell in Dumfriesshire, and founded there the first savings bank – to disprove the proposition that you cannot serve God and Mammon!

Dundas

From lands in West Lothian, the name is recorded from 1200. Henry Dundas, Viscount Melville (1742–1811) was a politically powerful Scots advocate and Secretary of State.

Dunlop

From lands in north Ayrshire, recorded from 1260. John Boyd Dunlop (1840–1921) was an Ayrshireman who invented the pneumatic tyre and gave his name to the Dunlop Rubber Company.

Dunn
Like **Brown** and **Black** and **White**, a surname from an adjective of colour: so the first Dunns had brownish or dun-coloured hair. A Thomas Dun was hanged in 1296 for stealing from the church in Elgin.

Duthie
Probably from Gaelic MacGille Dubhthaigh, 'son of the servant of Duthac', the patron saint of Tain. The surname is recorded from the 15th century.

Eddington, Edington
From the district near Chirnside, in Berwickshire, where the name is recorded from the 12th century.

Edmundston, Edmiston
From the hamlet or *tun* of Edmund, near Edinburgh, a name recorded from *c.*1200.

Elliot, Eliott, Eliot
A Border surname and clan name deriving from the Old English forename Aelfwald, later Elwald. With the **Armstrong**s, the **Kerr**s and the **Turnbull**s, the Elliots were defenders of the Scottish Marches, and like them became renowned as warriors. Jane Elliot (1727–1805) was a song writer best remembered for 'The Flowers of the Forest'.

Erskine
From the barony in Renfrewshire, the surname is recorded from the 13th century. John Erskine, 11th Earl of Mar (1675–1732), was known as 'Bobbing John' for for ever switching allegiance during the 1715 Jacobite uprising.

Ewart
From the village of Ewart, near Wooler in Northumberland. The surname is recorded mainly in Galloway from the 16th century. Ensign Ewart was the soldier who defended the Scottish colours at Waterloo and whose plaque is on the esplanade in front of Edinburgh Castle.

Ewing
An anglicization of Eoghann (or Ewan) recorded from the 16th century. **MacEwan** is a related name.

Fairbairn
Probably originally Freebairn, or Freeborn. The latter is recorded from 1150, Fairburn in 1327. Sir William Fairbairn (1789–1874) was an engineer who pioneered the use of steel in ship and bridge construction.

Fairweather
The etymology of the name is uncertain, but it is recorded from the 15th century.

Falconer
From the office of falconer, a trainer or breeder of falcons for sport, recorded from the late 12th century.

Farquharson
A branch of clan Chattan, descended from Farquhar, son of Shaw MacIntosh of Rothiemurchus in Strathspey. He was awarded lands at Braemar by Robert the Bruce for support against the Comyns. **Farquhar** in Old Gaelic is *fearchar* and means 'dear one'. Surnames **MacFarquhar** and MacKerracher and Farquhar are all related.

Fenton
From the prime agricultural lands of Fenton and Fenton Barns in East Lothian. John de Fenton was sheriff of Forfar in 1261.

Ferguson, Fergusson
Originally meant 'the son of **Fergus**', and rendered MacFergus or MacKerras in the Highlands. Robert the Bruce granted the lands of Kilkerran in south Ayrshire to Fergus, son of Fergus. Robert Fergusson (1750–74) was an Edinburgh poet.

Ferrier, Feriar
From two sources: the trade of blacksmith, or ironsmith (Old French *ferrier*), and the trade of ferryman. Recorded from the 14th century. Sir David Ferrier (1843–1928) was a pioneering neuropathologist.

Fife, Fyfe, Fyffe
A surname from the old shire and kingdom of Fife, recorded from 1296. Sir David Maxwell Fyfe (1900–67) was a politician and Lord Chancellor.

Findlater

From the lands of Findlater in Banffshire, recorded from the 14th century. Andrew Findlater (1810–85) was the editor of the first edition of *Chambers's Encyclopedia* (1859–68).

Finlay, Findlay

From the Gaelic personal name Fionnladh, which means 'fair hero'. Recorded from the 13th century. (See also **Mackinlay**.)

Fleming

Originally the surname was given to people from Flanders – the Flemings were active traders with the Scots. Baldwin the Fleming was sheriff of Lanark around 1150. Sir Alexander Fleming (1881–1955) was a bacteriologist and discoverer of penicillin, a native of Darvel in Ayrshire.

Fletcher

From two occupational sources: first, *flèchiers*, or arrow-makers, hence the Fletchers of Glenlyon who were suppliers of arrows to the MacGregors; second, from the job of flesher, or butcher. The name is recorded from the 14th century. Andrew Fletcher of Saltoun (1655–1715) was a Scots parliamentarian and opponent of the 1707 Union.

Flockhart

From an old Fife surname of Flucker, perhaps in turn derived from the Frisian name of Fokker. Fluckhart is recorded in Edinburgh from the 17th century.

Forbes

From lands in Aberdeenshire, originally pronounced as two syllables, as early records show: Forbays, Forbees and Forbace were alternative spellings. Recorded from the 13th century. The family became one of the most powerful in the north-east, in longstanding rivalry with their even more powerful neighbours, the **Gordons**. Duncan Forbes of Culloden (1685–1747) was a Scottish jurist.

Fordyce

From the lands of Fordyce in Banffshire, recorded from the 15th century. A sept of the **Forbes** clan.

Forrester

From the occupation of forestry-worker or forest-keeper, from Norman-French *forestier* and Latin *forestarius*. Adam Forrester was an Edinburgh alderman in the 14th century and owner of the manor of Corstorphine from 1373. Splendid monumental effigies of his family can still be seen in Corstorphine parish church. Forrester High School in Edinburgh is named after this family.

Forsyth

Probably from an Old Gaelic forename Fearsithe, which meant 'a man of peace'. Fearsithe Mag Uibne was bishop of Breifne in Ulster (died 1464). Bill Forsyth (1948–) is a successful Scottish film-maker.

Fraser

The original name was Norman-French de Frisselle or de Fresel, from their arms which bore the flower of the *freze* (Old French), or strawberry. The names Frasee and Fraser are recorded in East Lothian and Tweeddale from the 12th century. In the same century, a member of the family acquired the Highland lands of Lovat in Inverness-shire by marriage. The Lovat Frasers became a powerful Gaelic-speaking clan. The Gaelic form of the name Friseal is closer than the current English form to the Norman-French original. Other spellings are still found: Frizell, Frisselle and Frazer. Sir James G. Frazer (1854–1941) was a famous anthropologist and folklorist.

French, France

These surnames were originally borne by people from France, often recorded in early charters in the Latin form of Franciscus or Francus, but found as French from the early 13th century.

Fullarton, Fullerton

From lands near Troon in Ayrshire. There is a charter of 1283 of the lands of Fullarton and Gailes in the Kyle Stewartry from James the High Steward.

Galbraith

The name in Gaelic is Mac a Bhreatnaich (Mac-Bratney), and means 'the Briton's son'. The original Galbraith is thought to have been a Welsh or

Strathclyde Briton. The name is recorded from the 13th century. John Kenneth Galbraith (1908–89) was a famous Canadian economist, author of *The Affluent Society* (1958) and other classic texts.

Gall
The Gaels referred to non-Gaels as the Gall, rather as the Greeks called non-Greeks barbarians. The name is recorded in the Lowlands in the 14th century. The surnames Gault and Gauld have the same etymology. John Galt (1779–1839) of Irvine was author of *Annals of the Parish* (1821) and other successful fiction.

Galloway
Originally the name was taken by people from this district of south-west Scotland. It is recorded from the 13th century, sometimes as Galway.

Gatherer
Probably from the occupation of crop gatherer, a small farmer. Recorded from the 16th century.

Geddes
From lands in Nairn, recorded as a surname from about 1400. Jenny Geddes, in a famous historical episode, threw her prayer stool at the episcopalian bishop preaching in St Giles High Kirk in Edinburgh in 1637. Sir Patrick Geddes (1854–1932) was a famous town planner and polymath.

Gemmell, Gemmill
From the once popular forename of Gamel or Gamellus, common in 12th-century charters. Gammie is from the same source.

Gibson
Originally meant 'son of Gib', a diminutive of **Gilbert**. This popular forename gave a variety of surnames of which Gibson is now most widespread: Gibb, Gibbon, Gibbonson and **MacGibbon** are all from this source. Gibson is recorded from the 14th century. John Gibson Lockhart (1794–1854) was the biographer of Scott. Sir Alexander Gibson (1926–   ) is a popular Scottish orchestral conductor.

Gifford

In Norman-French *giffard* meant someone who was plump and jolly and fond of food. The earliest charter of the lands of Yester to the Gifford family dates from 1186. The village of Gifford in East Lothian is named after them.

Gilchrist

In Gaelic Gille Criosd, which means 'Christ's gillie or servant'. One of the first Gilchrists was the sculptor of St Martin's Cross on Iona, and there were two Gilchrist witnesses in the *Book of Deer* (12th century).

Gilfillan

In Gaelic Gille Fhaolain, which means St 'Fillan's gillie or servant'. Recorded from the 12th century.

Gillanders

In Gaelic Gilleanndrais, which means St 'Andrew's gillie or servant'. Recorded from the 12th century.

Gillespie

In Gaelic Gilleasbuig, which means 'the bishop's gillie or servant'. Recorded from the 12th century. James Gillespie (1726–97) was an Edinburgh snuff merchant who founded the Edinburgh school which bears his name.

Gillies

In Gaelic Gille Iosa, which means 'servant of Jesus'. Recorded from the 12th century.

Gilmour, Gilmore

In Gaelic Gille Moire, which means 'servant of the Virgin Mary'. Recorded from the 12th century.

Glass

A surname from a nickname. *Glas* is Gaelic for 'grey', so the original bearer of the name may have been a grey-haired man. In Gaelic *Mac ghille ghlaisan* means 'son of the grey(-haired) man' which is rendered as MacGlashan in English, so the Glasses and the MacGlashans are related. Recorded on Bute from the 15th century.

Gordon

An Anglo-Norman family settled in the lands of Gordon in Berwickshire in the 12th century, soon becoming an influential Border family. They were granted the forfeited lands of the Comyns or **Cumming**s in Aberdeenshire in the 14th century, soon becoming all-powerful in north-east Scotland (hence their clan chief's nickname 'Cock of the North'). General Gordon (1833–85), killed by the army of the Mahdi at Khartoum, was a popular Victorian military hero; his family were from Aberdeenshire. Gordonstoun and Portgordon on the Moray Firth are named after Sir Robert Gordon, who bought the Elgin estate in 1683.

Gow

From Gaelic *gobha* ('a smith'). Most clans and Highland communities had their smith, so the name has no clan association. Recorded from the 17th century.

Graham, Graeme, Grahame

The name of an Anglo-Norman family granted lands in Lothian in the 12th century by King David I. They acquired lands in Angus in the 13th century. The most famous of the 'Gallant Grahams' were James Graham, the 'Great Marquis' of Montrose (1612–50) and John Graham of Claverhouse (1649–89), or 'Bonnie Dundee', who both met execution in the royalist cause. Kenneth Grahame (1859–1932) was the Scots-born author of *The Wind in the Willows* (1908). The name derives from Old English *graeg ham*, or 'grey home'.

Grant

From French *grand*, meaning 'big' or 'eminent'. The Norman family of Le Grant had lands at Nottingham in the 11th century, and are recorded in Scotland at Inverness from 1258. Through marriage they acquired lands in Strathspey and around Loch Ness. It was Strathspey Grants who built the model village of Grantown-on-Spey in the early 18th century. Elizabeth Grant of Rothiemurchus (1797–1885) is remembered for her diaries, published as *Memoirs of a Highland Lady* (1898). Ulysses S. Grant (1822–85) was the 18th US President and commander of the Union army in the American Civil War.

Grassick
From the trade of *greusaich*, 'a cobbler or shoe-maker' in Gaelic. Recorded from the 16th century in Lochalsh.

Gray, Grey
From two possible sources: first, a nickname indicating hair colouring; second, from the town of Gray in Burgundy. Recorded from the 13th century.

Grier, Greer
A shortened version of Gregor, or **MacGregor**, recorded from the 16th century in Dumfriesshire.

Grierson
From the same origins as **Grier**, recorded in Dumfriesshire from the 15th century. Sir Robert Grierson of Lag, in Dumfriesshire (1655–1733), was a Jacobite laird. Sir Herbert Grierson (1866–1960) was a Scottish academic and literary critic. John Grierson (1898–1972) was a Scots-born film and documentary producer.

Gunn
The name is of uncertain Norse origin, and is borne by a clan whose territories were in Caithness and east Sutherland. Gunni, son of Olaf, was a Caithness chieftain mentioned in the 12th-century *Orkneyinga Saga*. Neil Gunn (1891–1973) was one of Scotland's greatest modern novelists, author of the classic *The Silver Darlings* (1941).

Guthrie
From the lands of Guthrie in Angus, recorded from the late 13th century. Dr Thomas Guthrie (1803–73) was a famous Free Church minister and social reformer who founded a number of non-sectarian 'ragged schools' for poor children in Edinburgh.

Haig
The name is thought to be from Old English *haga*, or French *haie*, a 'hedge or enclosure'. There were

Haigs at Bemersyde in Lower Tweeddale from 1400 to 1867. Earl Haig (1861–1928) was Commander-in-Chief of the British army in World War I.

Haldane
Probably from the lands of Hadden in Roxburghshire. The surname Hauden is recorded from 1165, and Haldane of Gleneagles is recorded paying homage in 1296. The name is related to Howden and Hadden. Elizabeth Sanderson Haldane (1862–1937) was Scotland's first female Justice of the Peace in 1920.

Hamilton
A surname from the English placename of Hambledon. Hameldone and Hameldun are recorded from 1272. The origins of the present ducal family go back to the Wars of Independence, when Bruce rewarded Walter de Hamildone with Comyn lands in Lanarkshire. These lands included the village of Cadyow, renamed Hamilton after the new proprietor of the district.

Harkness
A surname associated with Dumfries and Galloway. There were several Covenanters of this name including at least one who suffered execution (Thomas Harkness, 1685).

Harper
From the occupation of harper, an important musician in great families. There were several Harpers in the *Ragman Rolls* (1296). The office of harper was often hereditary, and endowed with land: which is the origin of present-day farms called Harpercroft and Harperfield.

Harrison
Originally 'son of Harry', recorded in Scotland in the 15th century. The name is commoner in England.

Hastings
A Norman family of this name settled in Angus in the 12th century.

Hay

Probably from Old English *haga*, or French *haie*, 'a hedge or enclosure'. (See also **Haig**.) There was a Norman family de la Haye. In the 12th century William de Haya acquired the fertile lands of Erroll in the Carse of Gowrie from King William the Lyon. The family became hereditary High Constables of Scotland.

Henderson, Henryson

Originally 'son of Henry', sometimes pronounced Hendry. The earlier form of the name was Henryson, which has now died out. The clan's Gaelic name is Mac Eanruig (MacKendrick). Alexander Henderson (1583–1646) was an important churchman of his day, three times moderator, who drafted the famous Solemn League and Covenant. Robert Henryson (*c.*1425–1508), schoolmaster in Dunfermline, was a celebrated poet.

Hepburn

From the lands of Hebburn in Northumberland. The family prospered in East Lothian from the 13th century. James Hepburn, Earl of Bothwell (*c.*1537–78) was briefly married to Mary Queen of Scots, but fell from grace for a variety of nefarious activities.

Heriot

From the lands of Heriot in Midlothian, recorded from the 12th century. George Heriot (1563–1624), or 'Jinglin Geordie', was the goldsmith and banker to King James VI, whose fortune founded George Heriot's School in his native city of Edinburgh.

Herries

The Norman family name of Heriz appears in 12th-century charters. By the 14th century it was fairly widespread in Galloway.

Hislop, Heslop, Haslop

A surname from a location, 'at the hazel-hope'. Recorded from the 15th century.

Hogg

A surname from a nickname: first, from the name of the animal; second, from Old English *hoga*, 'careful or prudent'. Of considerable antiquity, the name is recorded in England from the 11th century and in south-east Scotland from the 13th. James Hogg (1770–1835), 'the Ettrick shepherd', poet and novelist, is the best-known bearer of this name.

Home, Hume
Both names are pronounced as 'Hume', and are from lands near Coldstream in Berwickshire. Sir Alexander Home (died 1491) was the first Lord Home and the title was raised to an earldom in 1605. David Hume (1711–76), the philospher, always spelled his name with a *u*, while his brother John favoured the *o* version. Sir Alec Douglas-Home (1903–) was Prime Minister 1963–4.

Horsburgh, Horsbrugh
From the lands of Horsburgh in Peeblesshire, recorded from the 13th century.

Houston
From the lands of Houston in Renfrewshire. Recorded from the 13th century. Samuel Houston (1793–1863) was the American soldier-statesman of Scottish origin who achieved Texan independence from the Mexicans and gave his name to the US city which bears his name.

Howie
Probably from a diminutive of How, a version of **Hugh**. A fairly widespread surname from the 16th century.

Hunter
From the activity of hunting. Early charters record the Latin version *venator*. Hunterston in Ayrshire takes its name from a local family. John Hunter (1728–93) and his brother William (1718–83) were prominent and pioneering doctors, respectively a physiologist and an obstetrician.

Hutchison, Hutcheson, Hutchinson
Originally 'son of Hutcheon', a diminutive of **Hugh**. Recorded from the 15th century in Glasgow and Aberdeen.

Imrie

From the obsolete Old English personal name Amalric. Recorded from the 14th century. The equivalent English surname is Emery.

Inglis

Originally a racial name to indicate English people; *Anglicus* in Latin charters. Recorded from the 13th century. Elsie Inglis (1864–1917) was a pioneering female doctor, founder of a maternity hospital in Edinburgh. Pronounced 'Ingils'.

Innes

From the lands of Innes in Morayshire, partly surrounded by streams (from the Gaelic *innis*, 'an island'). The name and the clan date from the 12th century.

Irvine, Irving

From the town of Irvine in Ayrshire and the parish of Irving in Dumfriesshire. The names are both recorded from the 12th century and have become somewhat interchangeable. Washington Irving (1783–1859), the American author and creator of Rip Van Winkle, was the son of an Orkney-born father.

Jamieson, Jameson

Originally 'son of **James** or Jamie'. Common surnames in the west of Scotland from the 15th century.

Jardine

From the French for garden (*jardin*), so a surname from a location. Winfredus de Jardine was a charter witness of King David I *c.*1150. Gardyne is a related surname, although it is also local to a parish in Angus.

Jarvie

From the personal name Jarvis or Gervase. Recorded from the 16th century at Stirling. Bailie Nicol Jarvie was a Glasgow merchant and town councillor in Walter Scott's novel *Rob Roy* (1818).

Johnson

Originally 'son of **John**'. This name is recorded in Scotland from the 'Ragman Roll' (1296), but is not nearly as frequent as **Johnstone**.

Johnstone, Johnston

Listed 11th most frequent Scottish surname in 1990, derived from various placenames. There was a **John**'s town in Annandale from the 13th century, and a later one in Renfrewshire. St John's Town of Dalry (Kirkcudbright) has retained its early nomenclature. The medieval name of Perth was St John's toun, as any football supporter knows. These locations gave rise to the surname.

Keith

Originally from lands in East Lothian (Dalkeith, Keith-Humbie). A Lothian Keith married a **Fraser** heiress in the 14th century and acquired extensive lands in Banffshire and the north-east. The town of Keith is named after this family. In 1455 they were ennobled, becoming hereditary Earls Marischal of Scotland and chiefs of their clan. In 1593 the 5th Earl Marischal founded Marischal College in Aberdeen, part of the university.

Kennedy

The name came from Irish Gaelic and is first recorded in Carrick, from the 12th century. The clan supported Bruce against the Comyns, and James II against the Black Douglases, thus acquiring considerable power in the land. James Kennedy (1408–65) was bishop of St Andrews and adviser to James II. His daughter Kate provides an annual pretext for celebration by the students of St Andrews University, where he founded a college in 1455. John F. Kennedy (US President 1960–3) was descended from the Irish Kennedys.

Ker, Kerr

A Border surname recorded from the 12th century, from Old Norse *kjarr*, 'brushwood or a copse'. The Lothian branch of the family favoured Kerr, the Roxburgh branch Ker. The Kers of Cessford were Wardens of the Marches, and the Duke of Roxburghe is now their chief. The Kerrs of Fernie-hirst are represented by the Marquis of Lothian, who is also the chief of the clan. John Kerr (1824–1907) was a Scots physicist who discovered the magneto-optic effect.

Kidd, Kydd

Probably from Kit, diminutive of Christopher. The name is recorded in charters from the 12th century. Captain William Kidd (c.1645–1701) was a famous Scottish buccaneer and pirate.

Kilgour

From lands near Falkland in Fife, recorded from the 16th century. There is a Kilgour river in north Australia, named after a Scottish explorer of the territory.

King

This surname is recorded in Scotland from the 13th century. The name was not a royal one, and there is a theory that it derives from a person's role in a medieval pageant or morality play – hence names such as King, Pope, Lord, Page, Knight and Abbot, etc.

Kininmont, Kininmonth

From lands in Fife, recorded from the 13th century. People of this name settled in France in the 15th century where they were recorded as Quinemont and Guenemont.

Kinnaird

From lands in Perthshire, recorded from the 13th century.

Kinnear

From lands in Fife, recorded from the 13th century. The name was associated with Balmerino Abbey in the 16th century.

Kirkpatrick

A Dumfriesshire name, after a chapel dedicated to St **Patrick**, at Closeburn. Recorded from the 12th century.

Knox

From the lands of Knock (Gaelic cnoc, 'a hill'), near Renfrew, recorded from the 13th century. John Knox (1513–72), the great Scottish reformer, is the most celebrated bearer of this name.

Laidlaw

A Border surname recorded from the 14th century, mainly in Selkirkshire. William Laidlaw (1780–1845) was Sir Walter Scott's factor at Abbotsford, and his friend and confidant.

Laing

A variant of **Lang**, recorded from the 14th century. R. D. Laing (1927–89) was an eminent Scottish psychiatrist; he sprang to prominence with his revolutionary ideas about mental disorder with the publication of *The Divided Self* (1960).

Lamb, Lambie, Lammie

Lamb is a Norse personal name, and was recorded as a surname from the 13th century. Diminutives Lambie and Lammie are recorded from the late 13th and 16th centuries respectively. Lamb's House, in Leith, is a fine 17th-century merchant's house.

Lamond, Lamont

An Argyllshire (Cowal) clan, called MacEarcher in Gaelic. A member of the clan took the title 'Lawman' or Lamont/d in the 13th century. The Cowal Lamonts fell foul of the **Campbell**s, who massacred them in 1661, when the chief was obliged to remove from his Castle Toward seat (which had been razed) to Ardlamont, at the western end of the Kyles of Bute. In England and America, the name is pronounced Lamónt, with the stress on the second syllable instead of the first.

Lang

A surname from a nickname, from Old English *lang*, meaning 'long or tall'. It is recorded in Scotland from the 13th century, even earlier as a byname in English Saxon chronicles. Andrew Lang (1844–1912) was a famous folklorist and writer. Cosmo Lang (1864–1945) was a Scots-born archbishop of Canterbury.

Lauder

From the Leader water and Lauderdale in Berwickshire, recorded from the 13th century. The singer and entertainer Sir Harry Lauder (1870–1950) was the most famous bearer of this name.

Laurie, Lawrie

Shortened versions of **Laurence**, recorded from the 15th century. The name is immortalized by Annie Laurie, of Maxwelton in Dumfriesshire, in the 18th-century song.

Lawson

From 'son of Law', where Law was a shortened version of Lawrence. Recorded from the 14th century.

Learmonth

From the lands of Learmonth in Berwickshire, recorded from the 13th century. Thomas the Rhymer of Erceldoune (c.1220–97), the seer and storyteller, is also recorded as Thomas Learmont. The Russian poet Lermontov (1814–41) was of Scots extraction.

Leiper

A *leap* was a rush basket, so the early Leipers followed the trade of basket-maker. The name is recorded from the 12th century.

Leitch, Leach

From the Old English name for a doctor (and user of leeches), recorded in Scotland from the 14th century.

Lennie, Leny

This surname has two sources: first, the lands and pass of Leny below Ben Ledi in Perthshire; second, from two Orkney hamlets, on Harray and North Ronaldsay. The Perthshire name is recorded from the 12th century, the Orkney name from the 16th.

Lennox, Lenox

From the district of that name south of the Campsie Hills, recorded as Levenax till the 15th century. Lennoxtown in Dunbartonshire is named after the local family.

Liddell, Liddle

From lands in Cumberland and Roxburghshire, recorded from the 13th century. Eric Liddell (1902–45), the missionary and Olympic sprinter, was the most famous modern bearer of this name.

Lindsay

Originally a Norman territorial name, from Limesay north of Rouen, it acquired its modern spelling of Lindsay as a Norman administrative division of Lincolnshire. The first Scottish Lindsay was Sir Walter de Lindesaya whose father came to Scotland with King David I in the early 12th century. The family acquired the lands of Crawford in upper Clydesdale, becoming Earls of Crawford in 1398 and continuing in this title to the present time. Sir David Lyndsay of the Mount (c.1486–1555) was a poet and dramatist, author of *The Satyre of the Thrie Estaitis* (first performed in 1540).

Linklater

From Linklet Bay on North Ronaldsay (Orkney) and other Orkney locations of this name. The surname is recorded on Orkney from the 16th century and in Shetland and Aberdeenshire in the 17th. Eric Linklater (1899–1974) was a famous Orkney-born novelist and journalist.

Linton

A surname from various placenames: West Linton in Peeblesshire, East Linton in East Lothian, and Linton in Roxburghshire. Recorded from the 12th century.

Lister

Originally Litster, which was the Middle-English name for a dyer of cloth. (Compare **Baxter**, **Brewster**, **Dempster**.) Recorded from the 13th century.

Lithgow

Originally Linlithgow, the modern surname has abbreviated the placename from which it derives. Recorded from the 13th century. William Lithgow (1582–1645) of Lanark was an early Scots traveller in Europe, North Africa and the Middle East. His *Rare Adventures and Painful Peregrinations* was published in 1632.

Little

A surname originating in a nickname which stuck, Also recorded as Latin *parvus* and French *petit* in 13th-century documents. *Petit* yields the modern surname Petty. Some Littles may also have been **Liddells** (and vice versa).

Littlejohn see **Meiklejohn**.

Livingston, Livingstone
From lands in West Lothian, originally Leving's tun or villa Leving in Latin charters of the 12th century. David Livingstone (1813–73) was the greatest of the Scottish missionary explorers.

Lochhead
A local name indicating people who lived at the head of a loch. Recorded from the 13th century.

Lockhart
Two Norman brothers who made good in Scotland in the 12th century were Stephen and Simon Locard. Stephen's power-base was north Ayrshire where the town of Stevenston bears his name. Simon's centre of operations was Lanarkshire and the village of Symington carries his name. John Gibson Lockhart (1794–1854) was the biographer and son-in-law of Sir Walter Scott.

Logan
From lands near Cumnock in Ayrshire, and from placenames in Wigtonshire and Midlothian. Recorded from the 12th century.

Lorimer
From the trade of lorimer, or spur-maker, a specialist form of blacksmith. Recorded from the 13th century. Sir Robert Lorimer (1864–1929) was famous as an architect and conservationist.

Loudon
From the lands of Loudoun, near Darvel in Ayrshire, where Loudoun Castle was a substantial Norman power-base. The original placename may be Loudun in the Loire valley in France. The Scottish surname is recorded from the 12th century. John Loudon (1783–1843) was a pioneering Scots horticulturist.

Love
Probably from French *louve*, a 'wolf', and sometimes shown in Latin charters as *lupus*. The name is recorded in the present spelling from the 15th century. Lovell (originally meaning 'a little wolf') is from the same source.

Lumsden
From lands in Berwickshire, recorded as a surname from the 12th century.

Lyle, Lyell
From Norman-French L'Isle ('the island') or De Lisle, recorded in Scotland from the 12th century. Sir Charles Lyell (1797–1875) was a Scottish geologist whose *Principles of Geology* (1830–33) was an influential work.

Lyon
Probably from the glen and river Lyon in Perthshire, though some early bearers of the name could have been people from the French town of Lyon. Recorded from the 14th century in Scotland, in England from the 12th.

Mac-, Mc-
This is the Gaelic prefix meaning 'son of'. It was affixed to names of Gaelic origin, and the large number of these names extant even today reminds us that Gaelic was for long Scotland's dominant tongue. Similar prefixes were Fitz- in Norman-French (Fitzsimons, Fitzpatrick, Fitzgibbon) and O' in Irish Gaelic (O'Connell, O'Donovan, O'Driscoll). Not all Mac names in Scotland are Scottish: many Irish Gaelic names were also formed in this way and came into the west of Scotland in the 19th century (McGrath and McLaughlin, for example, are respectively Irish versions of **MacRae** and **MacLachlan**).

MacAdam
Gaelic Mac Adaim, 'son of **Adam**', recorded from the 12th century. A sept of the clan **MacGregor**. John Loudon MacAdam (1756–1836) of Ayr invented the 'macadamizing' system of roadmaking.

MacAlister
Gaelic Mac Alasdair means 'son of **Alexander**', recorded from the 15th century. The clan base was Kintyre and Arran.

MacAllan
Gaelic Mac Ailin means 'son of **Allan**', recorded from the 14th century. The MacAllans were septs of various

clans: **MacFarlane**, **MacDonald** of Clanranald, **Grant** and **MacKay**.

MacAlpine, MacAlpin
Gaelic Mac Ailpein means 'son of Alpin', recorded from the 13th century. King Kenneth MacAlpine succeeded his father Alpine as king of the Dalriada Scots in 834 and ruled a united Pictish–Scottish kingdom from 846.

MacAnce, MacAinsh
Probably from MacAngus ('son of **Angus**'), a surname which died out in the 17th century, which is when records suggest these derived names were spreading.

MacAra
Gaelic *ara* means 'a charioteer', so the name means 'son of the charioteer'. The village of Balmacara in Lochalsh takes its name from this sept of the **MacRae** and **MacGregor** clans.

MacArthur
Gaelic Mac Artair means 'son of Arthur', recorded from the 13th century. The clan base was Argyll, and MacArthurs long claimed chiefship of the **Campbell**s. US General Douglas MacArthur (1845–1912) was of Scottish parentage and served in the Philippines. His son General Douglas MacArthur (1880–1964) accepted the Japanese surrender in World War II and later served in Korea.

MacAskill
Gaelic Mac Asgaill means 'son of Asgaill', from an Old Norse name Asketl. A sept of the **MacLeod**s of Lewis, the name is recorded from the 16th century.

MacAulay
The name has two Gaelic sources: Mac Amhalghaidh (an Old Irish name) and Mac Amlaibh (from a Norse root). The first version of the name was based in Dunbartonshire, around Helensburgh, and is recorded from the 13th century. The second branch of the name was based on Lewis.

MacAuslan, MacAusland, MacAslin

The name meant 'son of Absalom' and is recorded from the 13th century, most frequently in Perthshire and Lennox. A sept of the **Buchanan**s. An Ulster branch is spelt McCausland.

MacBean, MacBain

Gaelic Mac Bheathain means 'son of Beathan', which some claim also gives **MacBeth**. The clan was based in Moray, and the surname is recorded from the 15th century.

MacBeth

Gaelic Mac bethad means 'son of life', which signified a man of religion. The famous Macbeth (1005–57) of Shakespeare became king of Scots after murdering King Duncan in 1040.

MacBrair

Gaelic Mac brathair means 'the friar's son', viewed by some as a reproach to a celibate order. There were MacBrair bailies and provosts of Dumfries from the 14th to the 16th centuries.

MacBrayne

Gaelic Mac a Briuthainn means 'son of the judge', and indicated a hereditary legal officer in the Western Isles. The surname is recorded from the 16th century. A sept of the **MacNaughton**s and **MacDonald**s.

MacCaig

Gaelic Mac Thaoig means 'son of Tadhg', the poet. The name is found in Galloway from the 15th century, and is a sept of the **Farquharson**s and the **MacLeod**s of Harris. The greatest modern bearer of the name (very appropriately) is the poet Norman MacCaig (1910–), winner of the Queen's Poetry Medal in 1990.

MacCall, Macall

Gaelic Mac Cathail means 'son of Cathal', and the name is recorded from the 14th century. A sept of the clan **MacAulay**.

MacCallum

Gaelic Mac Caluim means 'son of **Calum**', and the name is recorded in this form from the 17th century.

The clan base was Argyll. The name could also be derived from the older Gaelic MaolCholuim which means 'servant of Columba' and gives the name **Malcolm**.

MacCleery, MacChlery, MacClearie

Gaelic Mac Chleirich means 'son of the clerk' or 'cleric', an appointment which existed in many clans. The surnames date from the 14th century.

MacClure, MacLure

Gaelic Mac'ill'uidhir means 'son of the servant of Odhar', and the name is recorded in Galloway from the 16th century. Sir Robert McClure (1807–73) was an Irish-born naval admiral and Polar explorer.

MacColl

Gaelic Mac Colla means 'son of Coll', a name recorded in Argyll from the 17th century. A sept of the **MacDonald**s and the **Stewart**s of Appin.

MacColm, MacCollam, MacCollum

From Old Gaelic MaolCholuim which meant 'servant of Columba' and which also gave the forename **Malcolm**.

MacCormack, MacCormick

Gaelic Mac Cormaig means 'son of Cormack', a name recorded from the 12th century. John McCormack (1884–1945) was a great Irish tenor singer, which reminds us that many of these Gaelic names are found on both sides of the Irish sea.

MacCorquodale, MacCorkindale

The Gaelic Mac Corcadail or 'son of Corcadail' is from the Old Norse personal name *Thorketil* ('Thor's kettle or vessel'). The surname is recorded in Argyll from the 15th century.

MacCracken

A Galloway surname now also well entrenched in Ulster. Recorded from the 16th century, they are a sept of the **MacNaughton**s – some even say an etymological corruption of that name.

MacCrae see MacRae.

MacCrimmon

A sept of the **MacLeod**s, the Gaelic name derives in turn from Old Norse Hromund, 'famous protector'. Recorded on Skye and the Isle of Man from the 16th century. A family of MacCrimmons were hereditary pipers to the MacLeods of Dunvegan from the 16th to the 19th centuries.

MacCrindle

Gaelic Mac Raonuill means 'son of **Ranald**', and gives the now rare names MacRanald and MacRonald as well as the more widespread MacCrindle. The latter is recorded from the 15th century in Ayrshire and Galloway.

MacCulloch

A Galloway name of uncertain etymology recorded from the 13th century. John MacCulloch (1773–1835) was a noted geologist of the Western Isles. John Ramsay McCulloch (1789–1864) was a political economist.

MacCunn

A Galloway surname related to MacEwan, from Gaelic Mac Eoghain. Hamish MacCunn (1868–1916) was the famous Scottish composer of *Land of the Mountain and the Flood*. (See also **MacEwen**.)

MacDiarmid, MacDermid, MacDermitt

Gaelic Mac Dhiarmaid means 'son of **Diarmid**' and the name is found from the 14th century. Hugh MacDiarmid was the pen-name of the poet Christopher Murray Grieve (1892–1978).

MacDonald

After **Smith** and **Brown**, MacDonald was the third most frequently found Scots surname in 1990. As might be expected, it is a clan name of considerable antiquity, traceable back to **Donald**, son of Somerled, Lord of the Isles in the 12th century. The main branches of the clan – for long the most powerful in Scotland – are MacDonald of the Isles, MacDonald of Clanranald (in Moidart), MacDonald of Sleat, MacDonnell of Glengarry, and MacDonnell of Keppoch (in Lochaber). Smaller branches were MacDonald of Ardnamurchan and MacDonald of

Glencoe (victims of the 1692 massacre). MacDonalds were also powerful in County Antrim in Ulster. The clan suffered disproportionately under the Clearances, thousands of the name migrating to North America in the 18th and 19th centuries. Flora Macdonald (1722–90) was the Jacobite heroine and protectress of the hapless Bonnie Prince Charlie. Marshal MacDonald (1765–1840) was a French soldier under Napoleon, hero of Wagram (1809) and son of a Scots Jacobite schoolmaster. George MacDonald (1824–1905) was the author of *At the Back of the North Wind* (1871) and much other fiction for children and adults. James Ramsay MacDonald (1866–1937) was Britain's first Labour Prime Minister.

MacDonnell
An alternative spelling favoured by certain septs of the **MacDonalds**.

MacDougall, MacDougal
A clan with similar ancestry to the **MacDonalds**, tracing their origins to Dougal, son of Somerled, 12th-century Lord of the Isles. Their base was in Lorne, but they lost ground under Bruce, having family links with the Comyns. William McDougall (1871–1938) was an American psychologist.

MacDowell, MacDowall
A Galloway branch of the **MacDougalls**, recorded from the 13th century. Found also in Ulster. Edward MacDowell (1861–1908) was an American composer and pianist.

MacDuff
From Gaelic Mac Dubh, 'son of the dark one'. The historical authenticity of Shakespeare's MacDuff is suspect, but there was a clan MacDuff in Fife from the 12th century. The MacDuff Earls of Fife were crown-bearers to the Scots kings in the 13th and 14th centuries. The Fife family then died out, but the name had spread into the north-east – hence the fishing village of MacDuff on the Moray Firth.

MacEwen, MacEwan
From Gaelic Mac Eoghainn, 'son of **Ewan**', the name is recorded from the 12th century. The clan had bases in Cowal, Lennox and Galloway.

MacFadyean, MacFadzean, MacFadden
From Gaelic 'son of Paidean' or 'young Pat'. Recorded in Kintyre from the 14th century.

MacFarlane, MacFarlan, MacParland
Gaelic Mac Pharlain means 'son of Parlan', from the Old Irish personal name Partholon – in legend, the first Irishman. The name is recorded in Lennox from the 14th century, where the clan was related to the Earls of Lennox. The clan lands were in Arrochar and Loch Lomondside.

MacFarquhar
This Gaelic name means 'son of **Farquhar**' and is recorded from the 12th century. It was rendered into English as **Farquharson** from the 14th century and this is now the clan name. Pronounced 'MacFarcar'.

MacFetridge
From Gaelic Mac Pheadruis, 'son of **Peter**', recorded from the 16th century.

MacFie, MacPhie
This Hebridean name has an interesting etymology and is from Gaelic Mac Dubhsith, 'son of the black man of peace'. Dubside, Macdufthi and Macdoffy are in 12th-century charters – the last syllable would have been the stressed one. The name was sometimes anglicized as MacDuffie.

MacGibbon
Gaelic for 'son of Gibb, or Gibbon', diminutive forms of **Gilbert**. Recorded from the 15th century.

MacGill
From Gaelic Mac an ghoill, 'son of the stranger' or Lowlander. The name has Galloway associations and is recorded from the 13th century. A sept of the **MacDonalds**. James McGill (1744–1813) was a Scots-born fur trader in Canada, whose wealth endowed McGill University in Montreal (1821).

MacGillivray
From Gaelic Mac Gille bhrath, 'son of the servant of good judgment'. The name has associations with Mull and Argyllshire and is recorded from the 16th century.

MacGowan

From Gaelic Mac Ghobhainn, 'son of the black-smith'. Recorded in Nithsdale from the 14th century.

MacGregor

'Son of **Gregor**, or Gregory', a popular papal name in the Middle Ages. The name is recorded in Perthshire from the 12th century. The clan was outlawed 1603–61 and 1693–1784 and during these years many MacGregors changed their names. The clan chief Rob Roy MacGregor (1671–1734) is immortalized in Scott's novel *Rob Roy* (1817) as a picturesque Robin Hood figure.

MacHarg

A Galloway name recorded from the 15th century.

MacIldowie

From Gaelic Mac Gille dhuibh, 'son of the black lad', recorded on Iona from the 12th century.

MacIlraith, MacIlriach

From Gaelic Mac Gille riabhaich, 'son of the freckled lad', recorded in Galloway and the Highlands from the 14th century.

MacIlroy, MacElroy

From Gaelic Mac Gille ruaidh, 'son of the red-haired lad', recorded from the 14th century in Dumfries-shire and Ayrshire.

MacInnes

From Gaelic Mac Aonghais, 'son of **Angus**'. The clan territory was in Morvern and Ardnamurchan, and the name is recorded from the 15th century. Helen MacInnes (1920–   ) is a popular modern novelist.

MacIntosh, Mackintosh

From Gaelic Mac an toiseach, meaning 'son of the chief'. (Compare modern Irish *Taoiseach*, or Prime Minister.) As most clans were organized under a *toiseach*, there are several sources of the name MacIntosh, which is recorded from the 14th century. Charles MacIntosh (1766–1843) was a Glasgow chemist who devised and patented the water-proofing material which bears his name. Charles Rennie Mackintosh (1868–1928) was a famous Glasgow architect.

MacIntyre

From Gaelic Mac an t-saoir, 'son of the carpenter'. This small clan's lands were mainly in Argyll, and the name is recorded from the 14th century.

MacKay, MacKie

From the Gaelic MacAodh, 'son of Aodh', recorded from the 14th century and now the second commonest Mac surname in Scotland. Their lands were in Islay, Kintyre and north-west Sutherland. Lord MacKay of Clashfern (1928–) was the first Scots lawyer to become head of the English bar and Lord Chancellor of England (1987).

MacIver, MacIvor

From Gaelic Mac Iomhair, 'son of Ivar' (a Norse personal name). Recorded from the early 13th century. The MacIvor spelling is Sir Walter Scott's.

MacKellar

Gaelic Mac Ealair means 'son of Ealair' or Hilary, and the name is recorded from the 14th century in Argyll where they were a sept of the **Campbell**s.

MacKenzie

From Gaelic Mac Coinnich, 'son of **Coinneach**' or **Kenneth**. Recorded from the 13th century, Ross and Cromarty was the clan's power-base. MacKenny and MacKenna are related names. Alexander Mackenzie was the 18th-century author of *The Prophecies of the Brahan Seer*, which foresaw the construction of the Caledonian Canal, the Highland Clearances and the coming of the railway. Sir Compton Mackenzie (1883–1972) was the author of *Whisky Galore* (1947) and other successful fiction.

MacKinlay

From Gaelic Mac Fionnlagh, 'son of **Finlay**'. Recorded from the 16th century. The name was anglicized as **Finlayson**. William McKinley (1843–1901) was 24th US President, and claimed Scots ancestry.

MacKinnon

From Gaelic Mac Fhionghan, 'son of Fingan'. St Fionghan was a disciple of St Mungo. Legend traces the name to clan Alpin royal stock, and they are recorded from 1400 on Mull, Iona, Tiree and in Perthshire.

MacLachlan, MacLauchlin

From Gaelic Mac Lachlainn, 'son of **Lachlan**', recorded in the 13th century in Cowal and Lorn.

MacLaren, MacLauren

From Gaelic Mac Labhruinn, 'son of **Laurence**', recorded in Perthshire from the 13th century.

MacLaverty, MacLarty

From Gaelic Mac Fhlaitheartaich, 'son of Flaherty', recorded from the 12th century in Kintyre.

MacLean, MacLaine

From Gaelic Mac Gille Eoin, 'son of the servant of **John**', recorded from the 13th century. Their power-base was Mull and the castles of Duart and Lochbuie. The clan chief fell at Flodden protecting King James IV. Alistair Maclean (1922–87) was the author of a number of best-selling novels including *HMS Ulysses* (1955) and *Guns of Navarone* (1957).

MacLehose

From Gaelic Mac Gille Thamhais, 'son of the servant of Tammas', recorded from the 15th century. Robert Burns dedicated poems and songs to Mrs Agnes Maclehose (1759–1841) or 'Clarinda'.

MacLeish

From a shortened version of Gaelic Mac Gill'Iosa, 'son of the servant of Jesus'. Recorded from the 14th century. MacAleese is a related name.

MacLennan

From Gaelic Mac Gill-Finnein, 'son of the servant of Finnean'. Recorded from the 13th century, their main base was in Kintail.

MacLeod

From Gaelic 'son of Leod', an Old Norse name. The clan claims descent from the last Norse king of Man and the Hebrides, and has two main branches – Harris and Lewis. They soon acquired lands in Skye, Raasay, Assynt and Strathpeffer. Fiona MacLeod wrote modern versions of Celtic myths and legends, and was the pseudonym of William Sharp (1855–1905).

MacLullich

From Gaelic Mac Lulaich, 'son of Lulach', recorded from the 14th century mainly in Argyll. Some **MacCullochs** were really MacLullichs.

MacManus

From Gaelic Mac Maghnuis, 'son of **Magnus**', recorded from the 16th century in Dunbartonshire.

MacMaster

From Gaelic Mac Mhaighstir, 'son of the master', ie the priest, recorded in Argyll and Galloway from the 15th century.

MacMichael

From Gaelic Mac Gille Micheal, 'son of the servant of **Michael**', abbreviated to Mac Micheal. The fuller name is recorded from the 12th century, and the shortened version appears in the 16th. They are a sept of the **Stewart**s.

MacMillan

From Gaelic Mac Mhaolain, 'son of the tonsured one' (or bald one), an ecclesiastical name recorded from the 13th century. The clan lands were in Lochaber, Argyll and Galloway. Harold Macmillan (1894–1986) was a UK Prime Minister whose nickname was 'Supermac'.

MacMurchie, MacMurchy

From Gaelic Mac Mhurchaidh, 'son of **Murdo**', recorded from the 13th century.

MacMurdo

From the same source as **MacMurchie**.

MacMurray

A Galloway surname, from MacVurich (Gaelic *Mac Mhuirich*), recorded from the 12th century.

MacNab

From Gaelic Mac an Aba, 'son of the abbot'. The first clan chiefs were lay abbots of Glendochart in Strathtay. Recorded from the 14th century.

MacNaughton, MacNaughten, MacNachten

From Gaelic Mac Neachdainn, 'son of Nechtan'. Nechtan was a Pictish name: of a saint (died 679), a king of the Picts (died 732), and the battlefield of Nechtansmere in Angus. The surname is recorded from the 13th century.

MacNee

From Gaelic Mac neidhe, 'son of the champion', recorded from the 11th century.

MacNeil, MacNeal

From Gaelic Mac Niall, 'son of Nial', recorded from the 14th century. The clan had two branches – in Barra and Gigha. According to legend, the clan was descended via Aodh O'Neill (11th-century king of Ulster) from Niall, High King of Ireland.

MacNeish, MacNeice

From Gaelic Mac Naos, 'son of **Angus**'. Recorded from the 16th century. Louis MacNeice (1907–63) was an Ulster-born poet.

MacNicol

From Gaelic Mac Niocal, 'son of **Nicol**' (or Nicolas). Recorded from the 15th century. The name was early Englished as **Nicolson**.

MacPhail

Gaelic for 'son of **Paul**', recorded from the 15th century.

MacPhedran

Gaelic for 'son of little **Peter**', (Mac Pheadarain), recorded from the 14th century in Argyll.

MacPherson

Gaelic for 'son of the parson' (Mac a Phearsain), recorded from the 15th century. James MacPherson (1736–96) was a Highland schoolmaster, and author (he called himself 'translator') of the popular *Fingal, an Epic Poem* (1762) and other Ossianic works from Celtic legend.

MacQuarrie, MacQuarie

Gaelic for 'son of Guaire' (an Old Gaelic name which signified 'noble or proud'), recorded from the 15th century on Ulva and Mull. Lachlan MacQuarie (1761–1824) was a colonial administrator, governor of New South Wales, and sometimes called 'the father of Australia'. There are rivers Lachlan and MacQuarie in Australia, as well as MacQuarie Island.

MacQueen

Gaelic for 'son of Suine, or Suibhne' (an Old Gaelic name which signified 'well-going'), pronounced 'MacHuin' and recorded from the 15th century. MacSween is a related form. Loch Sween and Castle Sween in Knapdale are from the same name. Robert MacQueen, Lord Braxfield (1722–99), was a harsh, 'hanging' Scottish judge whose character was immortalized in Robert Louis Stevenson's *Weir of Hermiston* (1896).

MacRae

Gaelic for 'son of grace', this indicated an ecclesiastical origin and was an old personal name (like Macbeth) and not a patronymic. It is recorded from the 13th century. The clan's base was Kintail, and they were constables of Eilean Donan Castle.

MacRobb, MacRobbie, MacRobert

All these names are from Gaelic 'son of **Robert**' and its diminutives, and are found from the 15th century.

MacRorie, MacRury

Gaelic for 'son of Ruaridh, or **Rory**', recorded from the 13th century.

Macsporran, Macsparran

From Gaelic Mac-an-sporain, 'son of the purse', a name traditionally associated with the hereditary bursars or purse-bearers of the Lords of the Isles. Recorded from the 11th century.

MacSween see MacQueen.

MacTaggart

From Gaelic Mac-an-tsagairt, 'son of the priest', recorded from the 13th century. William McTaggart

(1835–1910) and his grandson Sir William MacTaggart (1903–81) were famous Scottish artists.

MacTavish
From Gaelic Mac Tamhais, 'son of Tammas', recorded from the 14th century.

MacTear
A shortened version of **MacIntyre**, recorded from the 14th century.

MacTurk
Gaelic for 'son of Torc' (*torc*='a boar'), recorded in Galloway from the 16th century.

MacVicar
Gaelic for 'son of the vicar', recorded in Argyll from the 15th century.

MacVitie, MacVittie
Of uncertain etymology, the name is recorded in Galloway from the 16th century.

MacWhinney
A form of **MacKenzie** recorded in Ayrshire and Galloway from the 16th century.

MacWhirter
From Gaelic Mac cruiteir, 'son of the harper', the clan harper often being a hereditary occupation in the Highlands. Recorded from the 14th century. John MacWhirter (1839–1911) was an artist of Highland scenes.

MacWilliam
From Gaelic for 'son of **William**', recorded from the 12th century. In the 16th century many bearers of the name took the English version of **Williamson**.

Mair
This name has the same etymology as *mayor* and *major*, and indicated first a court officer and later applied more widely to any delegated office. Recorded from the 13th century. John Mair, or Major (*c.*1470–1550), was a scholastic theologian and author of European renown, sometimes dubbed 'the last of the schoolmen'.

Maitland

Recorded in Scotland and Northumberland from the 12th century. William Maitland of Lethington (*c.*1528–73) was an adviser to Mary Queen of Scots.

Malcolm

From Old Gaelic MaolCholuim, 'servant of Colum' (or St Columba), recorded from the 11th century. Four early kings bore this name, which guaranteed its widespread use in Scotland. The clans Malcolm and **MacCallum** shared a common origin in Argyll.

Malloch

A Gaelic nickname from *mhallich*, indicating bushy eyebrows. Recorded from the 16th century.

Manson

A shortened form of the Norse name Magnusson ('son of **Magnus**'), common in Caithness and the Northern Isles from the 16th century. They were a sept of clan **Gunn**. Sir Patrick Manson (1844–1922) was a Scots doctor who did pioneering work on malaria: his nickname was 'Mosquito Manson'.

Manuel

From lands in Stirlingshire, originally from a priory called Emanuel. Recorded from the 13th century.

Marjoribanks

From lands in Renfrewshire, which got their name from the princess **Marjorie**, daughter of Robert the Bruce, when she married Walter the High Steward in 1316.

Marnoch

From lands in Aberdeenshire, near Huntly. Recorded from the 15th century.

Marr

From lands of Mar (Aberdeenshire) and Marr (Yorkshire), recorded in Scotland from the 13th century. Charles Kerr Marr was a Troon-born businessman who left money in 1919 to found Marr College, the town's secondary school.

Marshall

From French *maréchal*, a horse farrier or smith. The position of keeper or mareschal of the horses in a household was an important and often hereditary office. The name is recorded in Scotland from the early 12th century.

Martin

A surname from a popular personal name, recorded in Scotland from the 14th century.

Mason, Masson

From the trade of stonemason, from French *maçon*. Recorded in Scotland from the 13th century.

Masterton

From lands in Fife, near Dunfermline, recorded from the 13th century.

Mather, Maider

Of uncertain etymology, Madour was recorded in Fife from the 14th century, Mather from the 16th. The latter is probably local, from lands in Kincardineshire.

Matheson, Mathewson

Two origins: first, from 'son of **Matthew**', recorded from the 12th century; second, from Gaelic Mac Mhathain, meaning 'son of the bear', which is recorded from the 13th century and is also in the Norse sagas. The Gaelic name also survives as MacMath.

Mathie

From an Angus placename, recorded from the 15th century.

Maule

From a Norman name de Maules, from the seigneurie de Maule in upper Normandy. Recorded from the 12th century.

Mavor

From the Gaelic office of *maor*, related to Scots *mair* and English *major*. Recorded in Strathspey from the 15th century. O. H. Mavor (1888–1951) was a dramatist better known by his pseudonym, James Bridie.

Maxton

From the place in Roxburghshire, the tun of Maccus, a local Saxon landowner whose name is also preserved in Maccus's well (or **Maxwell**). Recorded from the 12th century. A Perthshire Maxton in the 18th century composed this prayer exhorting protection from over-powerful neighbours:

> From the greed of the Campbells,
> From the ire of the Drummonds,
> From the pride of the Grahams,
> From the wind of the Murrays,
> Good Lord, deliver us.

James Maxton (1885–1946) was chairman of the Independent Labour Party and a Glasgow MP (1922–46).

Maxwell

From the place by the Tweed near Kelso, the well of Maccus. (See also **Maxton**.) The clan lands were in Nithsdale and Wigtownshire. Their chief fell at Flodden, and they were frequent Wardens of the West Marches. The bonny braes of Maxwelton are immortalized in the song 'Annie Laurie'. James Clerk Maxwell (1831–79) was a physicist who articulated the theory of electromagnetic radiation.

Meek

A Fife name recorded from the 15th century, of uncertain etymology.

Meikle

A descriptive name, originally indicating a large or tall person, recorded from the 14th century.

Meiklejohn

Like Meikle, a descriptive name, meaning Big **John** – opposite of Littlejohn. Littlejohn and Meiklejohn are both recorded from the 15th century.

Meldrum

From the place in Aberdeenshire, recorded from the 13th century.

Melven, Melvin

Variants of **Melville**, recorded from the 12th century.

Melville

A Norman name, from the placename of Malleville (Pays de Caux). Recorded from the 12th century, the family had lands in Midlothian near Dalkeith.

Menzies

From a Norman name, de Meyners (Mesnières), recorded in Scotland from the 12th century. From the same Norman name in England came the surname Manners. The clan became established in Perthshire in the 15th century. Sir Robert Menzies (1894–1978) was an Australian Prime Minister of Scots origin. Scottish pronunciation is 'Ming'ies', while the English tend to follow the spelling when pronouncing this surname.

Mercer

From the Middle-English word *mercer*, a draper or trader. Recorded in Scotland from about 1200.

Merrilees

From lands beside the Binns, in West Lothian, recorded from the 16th century. Meg Merrilees was an old gypsy woman in Scott's novel *Guy Mannering* (1815).

Messer

From French *messier*, a small cultivator. Recorded from the 13th century.

Methven, Methuen

From lands in Perthshire, recorded from the 13th century.

Michie

The surname derives from a diminutive of **Michael**, and is recorded in Aberdeenshire from the 16th century. A sept of the **MacDonald**s of Keppoch.

Middlemiss, Middlemass

From lands near Kelso, recorded from the 15th century.

Mill

Perhaps a simplification of **Milne**, recorded from the 15th century. James Mill (1773–1836) was a

philosopher, editor and historian, and father of John
Stuart Mill (1806–73), the more famous philosopher
and radical reformer.

Milligan
From Gaelic Maolagan, 'the little bald or tonsured
one', recorded in Galloway from the 13th century.

Milne, Miln, Mylne
Originally indicated a person who lived near a mill,
from Old English *myln* and Latin *molina*. Recorded in
Aberdeenshire from the 14th century.

Milroy
A shortened version of **MacIlroy**, recorded in Ayrshire and Galloway from the 17th century.

Mitchell
From Norman–French Michel (**Michael**), recorded
from the 15th century. Sir Thomas Mitchell (1792–
1855) was a Scottish explorer of the Australian
interior.

Moffat, Moffatt
From the placename in Dumfriesshire, recorded as a
surname from the 13th century. Robert Moffat (1795–
1883) was a biblical scholar and missionary in South
Africa.

Moggach
From Gaelic *mugach*, 'grumpy', recorded in Strathspey from the 17th century.

Moir
From Gaelic *mor*, 'big', recorded in Aberdeenshire
from the 14th century. David Moir (1798–1851) was a
medical practitioner and was the author of the
humorous *Life of Mansie Wauch* (1828).

Moncrieff, Moncreiffe
From lands in Perthshire, recorded as a surname from
the 13th century.

Moncur
Of uncertain origin, possibly from Norman–French
(*mon coeur*='my heart'), recorded as a surname from
the 13th century.

Monro see **Munro**.

Monteith, Monteath
From Menteith in Perthshire, recorded from the 14th century.

Montgomery, Montgomerie
From the Norman castle of Sainte-Foi-de-Mont-gomerie, the name was carried into England, Wales (Montgomeryshire) and eventually reached Scotland in the 12th century. The clan's lands were in Ayrshire and Kintyre. Alexander Montgomerie (1545–1611) was a poet, author of *The Cherrie and the Slae* (1597).

Moodie, Moody
Perhaps from Old English *modig*, 'brave'. Recorded in Scotland from the 14th century.

Morgan
From Pictish *Morcunn* and from an Old Celtic personal name, derived from *mori-cantos* ('sea bright'). The latter was also taken into Welsh and Breton. In Scotland, the use of the surname was associated with clan **MacKay** in Sutherland, and with Aberdeenshire. Recorded from the 13th century.

Morrison, Morison
'Son of Maurice, or Morris', recorded from the 15th century. This is also the English rendition of Gaelic *Mac GilleMhuire* ('son of the servant of the Virgin Mary'), a clan whose main base was the Outer Hebrides. MacMorris is a related surname. Robert Morrison (1782–1834) was a Scots missionary in China who compiled a Chinese dictionary (1823).

Mortimer
From a Norman-French placename Mortemer, derived in turn from Latin *mortuum mare* ('dead sea'), a name given by some Celtic peoples to the North Sea. The name is recorded in Scotland from the 12th century.

Morton
From lands in Dumfriesshire and in Fife (Myreton), recorded from the 13th century. The Earls of Morton were a branch of the **Douglas** family, and the 4th Earl,

James Douglas (1525–81) was involved in the assassination of Rizzio (1566) and of Darnley (1567), and was himself beheaded.

Mowat, Mowatt, Mouat

From a Norman-French location (*Mont Haut*, 'high hill, or mountain'). The name is recorded in Latin charters as de Monte Alto, and is found in Scotland from the 12th century.

Moyes

From French Moïse (Moses), recorded in Scotland from the 13th century. Moyses was an early variant.

Muir, Moore, Mure

Originally indicated people who lived near a muir or heath. Not surprisingly in a country with such a lot of moorland, the surname is now among the 100 commonest in Scotland, and has been recorded from the 13th century. Sir John Moore (1761–1809) was a Scottish soldier who died at Coruna in the Peninsular War, and is immortalized in the poem 'The Burial of Sir John Moore', by Wolfe. Edwin Muir (1887–1959) was an important Scots poet.

Muirburn, Muirhead, Muirhouse

Names deriving from location on or by a heath or muir.

Munro, Monro, Monroe

The name appears to be of Ulster origin, but is recorded in Scotland from the 14th century. James Monroe (1758–1831), fifth US President, was of Scots–Irish origin. H. H. Munro (1870–1916) was a novelist and short-story writer, better known by the pseudonym of Saki. Sir Hugh Munro of Lindertis (1856–1919) compiled *Munro's Tables of the 3000 Feet Mountains of Scotland* (1891), the 'Bible' of Scottish hill climbers.

Murchison

From Gaelic Mac Mhurchaidh, 'son of Murchadh' (**Murdo**), recorded in the English form from the 15th century. Sir Roderick Murchison (1792–1871) was a geologist and geographer. The Murchison Falls on the Upper Nile in Uganda are named after him.

Murdoch, Murdock
This name derives from two Gaelic names: Muireach, 'a sailor'; and Murchadh, 'a sea warrior'. Recorded from the 12th century. William Murdock (1754–1839) was a Scots mechanical engineer and inventor of coal gas.

Murison
An Aberdeenshire surname recorded from the 15th century.

Murray
From the province of Moray (in Gaelic *Moireabh*, 'sea settlement') in north-east Scotland, on the southern shore of the Moray Firth. Recorded from about 1200, in Latin charters as Moravia. 'The Bonnie Earl o' Murray' is immortalized in song. John Murray (1745–93) was a successful publisher of the work of Byron, Thomas Campbell and others.

Mustard
A Fife surname recorded from the 16th century. Probably of Flemish origin.

Nairn, Nairne
From the place in north-east Scotland, recorded as a surname from the 14th century.

Naismith, Nasmyth, Naysmith
From the trade of knife-maker, or knife-smith, recorded in Scotland from the 15th century. Alexander Nasmyth (1758–1840) was a famous portrait painter (of Robert Burns and others).

Napier
From the office of keeper of linen, or napery. The name is recorded in England from the Conquest, and was in Scotland by the 13th century. John Napier (1550–1617) was the inventor of mathematical logarithms and of a pioneering calculator.

Neil, Neill, Neal
From the Irish Gaelic heroic forename Niall, which spawned a wide range of names including Njal (Norse) and Nigel. First recorded as a Scottish surname in the 13th century. Neilston, in Renfrewshire, was named after a local family. (See also **MacNeil** and **Nelson**.)

Nelson, Neilson

Neilson was originally 'son of **Neil**' (in Gaelic **MacNeil**), recorded in Ayrshire and Caithness from the 13th century. This surname is probably one source of the very similar Nelson, recorded in Edinburgh and Inverness-shire from the 15th century. James Neilson (1792–1865) was the Glasgow inventor of hot-blast iron foundries. Thomas Nelson (father 1780–1861; son 1822–92) were Edinburgh publishers and benefactors.

Ness

Probably a local name (Neas in Gaelic), from headlands like Buchan Ness, Buddon Ness, Fife Ness, etc. Also the river Ness and Loch Ness (from Old Celtic *nesta*, roaring river). Recorded from the 12th century.

Newbiggin, Newbigging

A local name, from new farm biggins or buildings. Recorded from the 13th century.

Newton

A local name, from lands in Midlothian and Ayrshire.

Nicol, Nicoll

From the same source as **Nicolson**.

Nicolson, Nicholson

Son of **Nicol**, diminutive of Nicolas, which was a forename introduced into England and Scotland by the Normans. In Gaeldom it gave the related name MacNeacail (**MacNicol**). Recorded from the 13th century.

Nimmo

Of uncertain etymology, recorded in Scotland from the 15th century.

Nisbet, Nesbit

From the lands of Nesbit, Berwickshire, recorded from the 12th century.

Niven

From Gaelic *Naomhin*, 'little saint', once a popular forename. Recorded as a surname from the 13th century.

Noble
Probably of English origin, recorded in East Lothian from the 12th century.

Norval
An abbreviation of Normanville, placenames in Normandy. The full form was recorded in the 13th century, Norvyle in the 14th, Norwald in the 16th.

Ogg
From Gaelic *og*, 'young', recorded from the 15th century.

Ogilvie
From lands in Angus, near Glamis. The surname is recorded from the 12th century. The Ogilvies were Earls of Airlie from the 17th century, and were descended from the Celtic Earls of Angus. St John Ogilvie (1579–1615) was a Scottish Jesuit priest and martyr.

Oliphant
The name has a Norman-French origin, and was first recorded as Olifard, an olive grower. (See also **Oliver**.) The spelling and pronunciation of this name is said to have been affected by stories brought home by crusaders about that then unheard-of and fabulous beast – the elephant. Olifard is recorded from the 12th century, Olephant from the 17th.

Oliver
From the popular French forename, after one of Charlemagne's officers, brought to Scotland by the Normans. Recorded as a Scottish surname from the 12th century. In French, the name is also linked with the olive tree.

Orr
Probably from Gaelic *odhar*, 'sallow'. The surname Ure may be of similar origin. Recorded in Renfrewshire from the 13th century.

Orrock
From lands in Fife, recorded from the 13th century.

Osborn, Osborne
From Norse *Asbjorn*, 'god-bear', recorded from the 11th century.

Osler

From the occupation of ostler, stable-keeper, or innkeeper (Old French *hostelier*). Recorded from the 15th century.

Pagan

Once a popular forename, which signified a country person (rather than a townsman). From Latin *pagus*, a village or country district. The modern meaning stems from the notion that country people were slow to accept new ideas, including Christianity. Recorded as a surname from the 13th century.

Page

From the occupation of page, the personal servant of a knight. Recorded from the 13th century. (See also **King**.)

Palmer

Crusaders and pilgrims once wore palm-shaped leaves to show that they had been to the Holy Land, so the original Palmers had this distinction. Recorded in Scotland from the 13th century.

Paris, Parris

The name originally indicated people who came from Paris, and is recorded from *c*.1200.

Park

From lands in Renfrewshire, recorded from *c*.1200. Mungo Park (1771–1806), the West African explorer, was born in Selkirkshire.

Parker

From the occupation of park-keeper, recorded from the 13th century. Perhaps a park-keeper had to be nosy, in order to frustrate poachers – hence 'nosy parker'?

Paterson, Patterson

Son of **Patrick** (in Gaelic *MacPhadruig*). Recorded from the 15th century and now one of the 100 commonest Scottish surnames. William Paterson (1658–1719), the Scots financier, survived a leading involvement in the Darien disaster to found the Bank of England. Robert Paterson (1715–1801) was a Borders stonemason, the original 'Old Mortality' of Scott's novel of that title (1816).

Paton
Derived from Pat, a pet form of **Patrick**. Recorded from the 15th century. Pateman had a similar origin.

Pattullo, Patillo
From Pittilloch, a placename in Fife and Perthshire. Recorded from the 13th century.

Paxton
From lands in Berwickshire, recorded from the 13th century.

Peacock
From the name of the exotic bird, perhaps acquired by someone who kept them. Recorded in Scotland from the 13th century.

Peat, Peet
From Pete, a pet form of **Peter**. Recorded from the 15th century.

Peddie, Peattie
Diminutives of Pete, so they are really double diminutive names. Recorded from the 15th century.

Peebles
From the town and county, recorded as a surname from the 14th century.

Petrie
From a diminutive of **Patrick**, recorded as Patre and Petre from the 16th century.

Pickard
Originally referred to people from Picardy in northern France. Recorded from the 13th century.

Pinkerton
From lands near Dunbar in East Lothian, recorded from the 13th century. Allan Pinkerton (1819–84), founder of the American detective agency which bears his name, and head of the US secret service, was born in Glasgow.

Pirie
From a diminutive of French Pierre (**Peter**). Recorded from the 15th century.

Pitcairn
From lands in Fife, recorded from the 15th century. Pitcairn Island, in the South Pacific, was named after its 1767 discoverer, Robert Pitcairn, RN.

Pollock, Pollok
From estates in Renfrewshire, now part of Glasgow, recorded from the 12th century.

Porteous
Perhaps from French *pertuis* ('a narrow gap, or pass'). Recorded in the 15th century as Pertus, Portwis, etc. The Porteous Riots (1736) were a serious civil disturbance in Edinburgh following a public execution. John Porteous, captain of the town guard, ordered his soldiers to fire into the crowd. Six people were shot dead and the infuriated mob later hanged the hapless Captain Porteous.

Porter
From the occupation of porter or door-keeper of a castle or other important building. (See also **Dorward**.) Recorded from the 12th century. In the Highlands, Porters were also ferrymen (from Gaelic *portair*).

Potter
From the occupation of pot-maker, recorded from the 14th century.

Pottinger
From the occupation of cook or (French) *potager*, a maker of pottage or soup. Recorded on Orkney from the 15th century.

Prentice
From the position of apprentice, usually a young man bound to a master to learn his craft. Recorded from the 18th century.

Preston
From the lands of Preston, now Craigmillar Castle, Edinburgh. Recorded from the 13th century.

Members of the family also left their name at Prestonpans, where there were saltworks, and at Preston Mill in East Lothian.

Pringle
Abbreviated from lands of Hopringle in Roxburghshire. The full name is recorded from the 13th century, and the shortened modern form from the 15th.

Proctor
A shortened version of the title of procurator, which meant a manager or agent. Recorded from the 15th century.

Purdon
From French *prudhomme*, 'a man of worth, or a brave man'. Recorded from the 14th century.

Purves, Purvis
From French *parvis*, 'a church entrance', where various kinds of secular business were once transacted. Recorded in the Borders in the 13th century.

Quin, Quinn
From Irish Gaelic *Mac Cuinn*, 'son of Conn'.

Rae
A Borders surname, recorded in Dumfriesshire from the 13th century. John Rae (1831–93) was an Arctic explorer and came from Orkney.

Raeburn
From lands of Ryburn in north Ayrshire, recorded from the 14th century. Sir Henry Raeburn (1756–1823) was a celebrated Edinburgh portrait painter.

Ramsay
Of English territorial origin, from Ramsey, in Huntingdonshire. Recorded in Midlothian from the 12th century, where Dalhousie Castle became the family's power-base. Allan Ramsay (1685–1758) was a poet and pioneer librarian in Edinburgh, living at Ramsay Lodge (now Ramsay Garden) on Castle Hill. His son, also Allan (1713–84), was a famous portrait painter.

Rankin, Rankine, Ranken

From an obsolete diminutive forename, probably of Randolph. Compare Jankin, Lambkin, Peterkin. Recorded from the 15th century.

Reid, Reed

A surname from a nickname, 'red-haired or ruddy'. Recorded from c.1200. John Reid (1721–1807) was a Scots general and musician who endowed the chair of music at Edinburgh University.

Rennie, Rainey

From a diminutive of Reginald, recorded from the 14th century. John Rennie (1761–1821) was a great civil engineer and builder of bridges, canals and harbours.

Riach, Reoch

From Gaelic *riabhach*, 'greyish-haired or grizzled'. Recorded from the 15th century.

Riddell, Riddall

From Ryedale in north Yorkshire, recorded in Scotland from the 12th century.

Ritchie

A common Borders name, from Richie, a diminutive of **Richard**. Recorded from the 15th century.

Roberton

From lands in upper Clydesdale, recorded from the 13th century.

Robertson

Son of **Robert**, recorded from the 14th century. The Gaelic clan name was Donnachaidh or Donnachie, but c.1500 it adopted the new name of Robertson from a clan chief named after Robert the Bruce. William Robertson (1721–93) was a historian and principal of Edinburgh University.

Robinson

Son of **Robin**, recorded from the 15th century.

Rogerson, Rodgerson

Son of Roger, recorded from the 13th century.

Romanes
From lands in Peeblesshire, now Romanno Bridge. Recorded from the 13th century.

Rose
A small clan related to the **Ross**es, based around Nairn.

Ross
From Gaelic *ros*, a promontory, and the lands of Easter Ross around the Cromarty Firth; or from French *roux*, 'red-haired'. There was a Norman family de Ros in north Ayrshire by the 12th century. Sir John Ross (1777–1856) was a Scots explorer of the Arctic and the North West Passage.

Rutherford
From lands in Roxburghshire, from Old English *hrythera ford*, 'the ford of the cattle' (compare Oxford). Recorded from the 13th century. They became a powerful Border family. Daniel Rutherford (1749–1819) was a Scottish physician and botanist, discoverer of nitrogen (1772).

Ruthven
From lands in Angus, recorded from the 13th century. The Earls of Ruthven were implicated in a plot to kidnap King James VI at Perth. The name was outlawed in 1600.

Salmon, Salmond
From the forename Solomon, via Salamon. The *d* is intrusive, as in Henry/Hendry. Recorded from the 12th century.

Sanderson, Saunderson
Sander's son, or Saunder's son, from diminutives of **Alexander**. Recorded from the 15th century.

Sandeson, Sandison
Sandy's son, from a diminutive of **Alexander**. Recorded from the 15th century.

Sangster
From the office of sangster (singer) or chorister. There were sang schools in a number of cathedral towns including Aberdeen, where the surname is recorded from the 15th century.

Scott

A racial name borne originally by people from north of the Forth (the Scoto–Pictish kingdom). Uchtred filius Scoti ('son of a Scot') was the first recorded bearer of the name in 1124 and was probably the founder of the clan, with branches of Buccleuch in the Borders and Balwearie in Fife. Michael Scot (c.1175–1230) was a celebrated medieval scholar and astrologer, a 'wizard' according to some of his contemporaries (such as the poet Dante). Sir Walter Scott (1771–1832), Scotland's greatest man of letters, was the most famous bearer of this name, and was descended from one of the family's Border branches.

Scrimgeour

From *skrymsher*, the Middle-English word for 'a fencer, or skirmisher', recorded from the 13th century. The family held the office of Constables of Dundee Castle, and according to Boece's *Chronicles* (1526) they were also royal standard-bearers.

Sellar

From *seler* (Middle English) and *sellier* (French), 'a saddler'. Recorded from the 13th century.

Semple, Sempill

From French Saint-Paul, used as a placename; and from the nickname 'simple'. Robert Sempill (1595–1665) was a poet and songwriter, as was his son Francis (c.1616–82).

Seton

From lands in East Lothian, recorded from c.1150. Mary Seton was one of the Four Marys of Mary Queen of Scots.

Shand

A surname recorded in north-east Scotland from the 16th century.

Shanks

From a nickname, the Scots word for legs (compare **Cruikshank**), recorded as a surname from the 14th century. King Edward I of England was given the sobriquet Longshanks by Scots. Shanks of Barrhead were for long a byword for toilet fittings. 'Shanks's pony' is an idiomatic expression meaning 'on foot' (as in 'The car broke down so we had to complete our journey on Shanks's pony').

Shannon, Shennan
From Gaelic *seanáin*, 'a wise old man' or 'elder'. Recorded from the 14th century.

Sharp, Sharpe, Shairp
Like Smart, a surname from a nickname, recorded from the 14th century. James Sharp (1613–79) was an ill-loved episcopalian archbishop of St Andrews who came to a sticky end.

Shaw
The Lowland source of this name was local, from shaw or schaw, 'a woodland', as in Pollokshaws (Glasgow). Recorded as a surname from the 13th century. The Highland Shaws – or Shiachs – were a branch of clan Chattan. The name was from *sithech*, an Old Gaelic word for a wolf, and was recorded in the *Book of Deer* (12th century).

Shearer
From the occupation of shearing sheep. Recorded from the 14th century.

Shepherd, Sheppard
From the occupation. Recorded from the 14th century.

Sheriff
From the legal office of sheriff, or *shire-reeve*. Recorded from the 14th century.

Sheil, Shiel, Shields, Shiell
From a diminutive term for a shepherd's bothy, or *sheiling*. Recorded from the 14th century.

Shivas, Chivas
From lands near Tarves in Aberdeenshire. Recorded from the 14th century.

Sibbald
From Old English personal names Saebeald and Sigebeald ('sea bold' or 'victoriously bold'). Recorded

from the 13th century. Sir Robert Sibbald (1641–1722) was an Edinburgh naturalist and physician.

Sillar, Sillars
Probably from the occupation of silversmith, recorded from the 17th century.

Sim, Sime, Syme
From diminutives of Simon/Symon, recorded from the 15th century. James Syme (1799–1870) was an eminent Edinburgh surgeon and professor of clinical surgery.

Simson, Simpson, Symson
From 'son of **Sim** or Sym', recorded from the 15th century. Sir James Y. Simpson (1811–70) was a pioneer of obstetrics and professor of midwifery at Edinburgh University.

Sinclair
A surname derived from the Norman placename of Saint-Clair-sur-Elle, near Pont l'Evêque. Recorded in Scotland from the 12th century, at Roslin Castle in Midlothian. A branch of the family became Earls of Orkney and later of Caithness where, in true feudal fashion, many of their tenants took the surname of the overlord. Sinclair is now in the 80 most frequently found Scottish surnames. Sir John Sinclair (1754–1835) of Thurso was an agricultural improver, and compiled the *First Statistical Account of Scotland* (1791–9).

Sivewright, Sievewright
From the occupation of sieve-maker, recorded from the 16th century.

Skene
From lands in Aberdeenshire, recorded from the 14th century.

Skinner
From the occupation of skinner of animal hides. Recorded from the 13th century.

Small, Smail
From a nickname, recorded from the 14th century.

Smith

From the occupation of smith, or blacksmith, now the most frequently found of all names in Scotland. Recorded from the 12th century. Adam Smith (1723–90) was an economist and author of *Wealth of Nations* (1776). Iain Crichton Smith (1928–) is a poet, novelist and short-story writer.

Smollett

Of uncertain etymology, a surname recorded from the 15th century. Tobias Smollett (1721–71) was a novelist, author of *Roderick Random* (1748), *Humphrey Clinker* (1771) and other picaresque fiction.

Snodgrass

From lands called Snodgers or Snodgrass, near Irvine in Ayrshire. Recorded from the 14th century.

Somerville

A Norman name, recorded in Scotland from *c.*1200. Mary Somerville (1780–1872) was a Scottish mathematician and scientific writer. Somerville College, Oxford, is named after her.

Soutar, Souter

From the occupation of soutar, a shoe-maker or cobbler. Recorded from the 13th century. Souter Johnny is immortalized as Tam o' Shanter's drouthy crony. William Soutar (1898–1943) was a poet who wrote in Scots. According to legend, the Sutors of Cromarty, the two headlands guarding the entrance to the Cromarty Firth, were the workstools of two giant shoe-makers who supplied outsize footwear to their fellows.

Spence, Spens

From the office of keeper of household provisions (from dispenser). Recorded from the 13th century. Sir Basil Spence (1907–76) was the distinguished Scottish architect of Coventry Cathedral (1951).

Spottiswood

From the lands of Spottiswood, near Gordon, in Berwickshire. Recorded from the 13th century. John Spottiswood (1565–1639) was archbishop of St Andrews.

Sprott, Sproat
Surnames of Scandinavian origin, recorded from the 13th century.

Steedman, Steadman
Originally a man from a *stead*, or farmstead. Recorded from the 14th century.

Steel, Steele
From a variety of placenames, recorded from the 13th century. Sir John Steell (1804–91) was a famous sculptor.

Stevenson
Son of **Steven**, recorded from the 14th century, now among the 100 most frequently found Scottish surnames. From the same source come also Steen, Stein, Steinson, Stiven, and of course Steven, Stevens, Stephen, Stephens. Robert Stevenson (1772–1850) was a great lighthouse engineer, and his grandson Robert Louis Stevenson (1850–94) was the author of many classic texts, including *Treasure Island* (1883), *Kidnapped* (1886), *The Strange Case of Dr Jekyll and Mr Hyde* (1886), and *Weir of Hermiston* (published posthumously in 1896).

Stewart, Stuart, Steuart
A surname from the occupation of steward, or chief of the household (from Old English *stig-ward*, 'the warden of the sty'). In some households, this title became hereditary, notably in the royal house which in 1153 gave Walter the office of High Steward of Scotland. In 1315, Walter, the sixth High Steward, married Marjorie, daughter of King Robert the Bruce, and their son became King Robert II in 1371, thus establishing the name of Stewart as the Scottish royal house for the next 350 years. Mary Queen of Scots opted for the Stuart spelling while resident in France. Dugald Stewart (1753–1828) was a Scottish philosopher of the 'common-sense' school. John McDouall Stuart (1815–66) was a Scots-born explorer of Australia: Mount Stuart is named after him.

Stoddart, Stoddard
From the occupation of *stot-herd*, a person who looks after the stots or bullocks. Recorded from the 14th century. Thomas Stoddart (1810–80) was a poet.

Strachan, Straughan
From the lands of Strachan (pronounced 'Strawn') in Kincardineshire. Recorded from the 13th century. Douglas Strachan (1875–1950) was an artist who did much fine work in stained glass.

Strang, Strange
Originally indicated either a stranger, or a strong man. Recorded from the 13th century. Sir Robert Strange (1721–92) was a famous line engraver.

Stronach
An Aberdeenshire surname from a nickname, from Gaelic *sronach*, 'nosy'. Recorded from the 15th century.

Struthers
Originally a person who lived beside a *strother*, 'a marsh or a swamp' (Old English). Recorded from the 16th century.

Sutherland
Originally a person from the county of Sutherland. Recorded from the 14th century. Dame Joan Sutherland (1926–   ), the Australian operatic soprano, must have had a far-off ancestor from the north of Scotland: perhaps via Forbes Sutherland, an Aberdeenshire sailor, the first Briton buried on Australian soil (May 1770).

Swain, Swaine
From *Sveinn* (modern Sven), a popular Scandinavian forename. Recorded in Scotland from the 12th century.

Swan, Swann
This is a variant of **Swain**, recorded from the 12th century. Annie S. Swan (1860–1943) was a popular novelist.

Swinton
From lands in Berwickshire, recorded from the 13th century.

Sword
From the old forename Siward. It was Siward who defeated Macbeth at the hill of Dunsinane. The surname is recorded from the 14th century.

Tait, Tate

This was originally a nickname, meaning 'glad or cheerful' in Old English. Recorded from the 14th century.

Tannahill

From a placename, near Kilmaurs in Ayrshire. Robert Tannahill (1774–1810) was the Paisley poet of 'The Braes of Gleniffer'.

Taylor

From the occupation, 'a cutter of cloth', from Old French *tailleur*. Recorded from the 13th century.

Telfer

From French *taillefer*, 'cut iron', originally someone who worked iron. Recorded from the 13th century. (It is interesting to note that the German equivalent Eisenhauer also gave a surname, borne by US President Dwight D. Eisenhower, 1890–1969.) Telford is a variant spelling. Thomas Telford (1757–1834) was the great road-builder and engineer of the Caledonian Canal, the Dean Bridge in Edinburgh, the Menai Bridge in north Wales, and St Katherine's Dock in London.

Tennant, Tennent

Originally from *tenant*, the temporary occupant of a building or piece of land. Recorded from the 14th century. William Tennant (1784–1848) was the Fife poet of 'Anster Fair'.

Thin, Thyne

An Old English forename, and not a nickname. Recorded in Scotland from the 15th century. James Thin Bookshops have been in Edinburgh since the mid-19th century.

Thom

From a diminutive of **Thomas**, recorded from the 15th century.

Thomson

From 'son of Thom', a very popular medieval Christian name. Now the sixth most frequently found Scottish surname. Recorded from the 14th century.

There were two poets called James Thomson: one (1700–48) is best known for *The Seasons* (1730) and *The Castle of Indolence* (1748); the other (1834–82) had the pseudonym B.V. (Bysshe Vanolis, from the names of Shelley and Novalis) and is best remembered for *The City of Dreadful Night* (1874–80). David Couper Thomson (1861–1954) founded the D. C. Thomson newspaper business in Dundee.

Tindall

From the district of Tynedale in Northumberland, once part of Scotland. Recorded from the 13th century.

Todd, Tod

From the old nickname for the fox. Recorded as a surname from the 13th century. Alexander Todd (1907–   ) is a Scots chemist, awarded the Nobel Prize for chemistry for work on vitamins B and E.

Torrance

From placenames in Stirlingshire and Lanarkshire. Recorded from the 16th century.

Toshack

Recorded from the 13th century. From Gaelic *toiseach*, 'chief or leader'. Compare the modern Irish title of *Taoiseach*, or Prime Minister. (See also **MacIntosh**.)

Trotter

From French *trotier*, 'a runner, messenger or trotter'. Recorded in Berwickshire in the 14th century.

Tulloch

From lands near Dingwall in Easter Ross (from Gaelic *tulich*, 'a little hill'). Tullo and Tullis are variant spellings. Recorded from the 14th century. John Tulloch (1823–86) was a Scottish academic theologian.

Turnbull

From Old English *trumball*, 'strong or bold'. Recorded from the 14th century. There is also a legend of King Robert the Bruce being saved from a wild bull by one of his subjects who 'turned the bull' away, but there is no evidence to support this.

Turpin
From Old Norse Thorfinn, one of the Norse gods, via Norman French. Recorded in Scotland from the 12th century.

Tweedie
From lands in Lanarkshire, recorded from the 13th century.

Tyrie
From lands in Perthshire, recorded from the 13th century.

Urquhart
From lands in Inverness-shire, from Brittonic *air* ('upon'), *carrden* ('the woodland'). Recorded from the 14th century. King Robert the Bruce bestowed on William of Urquhart the hereditary sheriffdom of Cromarty. Sir Thomas Urquhart (1611–60) was the first translator of the works of François Rabelais into English.

Usher, Ussher
From the office of usher or door-keeper of the royal apartments, recorded from the 13th century. (See also **Dorward**.)

Veitch
Probably from French *vache* ('cow'), so originally someone who kept cows. Recorded from the 12th century.

Waddell, Weddell
From an earlier name for the lands of Stow, by Gala Water in Borders Region. Recorded from the 13th century.

Waddie, Waldie
Originally these names were diminutives of Waldeve, an Old English personal name recorded in Scotland from the 12th century but now defunct. The diminutive forms have flourished, and are recorded from the 16th century.

Walker
From the trade of *walker*, Old English for a fuller or finisher of cloth. Recorded from the 14th century. Sir James Walker (1863–1935), was a Scots chemist, noted

for pioneering work on hydrolysis, ionization and amphoteric electrolytes. John Walker of Kilmarnock founded a famous whisky brand, 'still going strong'.

Wallace

From Wallenses, a racial name indicating a Welsh Briton, probably from Strathclyde. Recorded from the 12th century. The great patriot, William Wallace (c.1274–1305) expelled the English from Scotland in 1297 in the Wars of Independence, but was ultimately captured and hanged by them.

Walsh, Welsh

From Old English *welisc*, indicating 'a foreigner'. Recorded from the 14th century. Jane Welsh (1801–66) was the patient wife of Thomas Carlyle (1795–1881).

Wardlaw

From various placenames in Scotland. Henry Wardlaw (c.1378–1440) was bishop of St Andrews and founder of its university (1411).

Wardrop

From the office of keeper of the wardrobe to the king. Recorded from the 13th century.

Warrender

From the office of *warrener*, keeper of a game park, literally a person who warned. (Compare **Parker**.) The *d* is intrusive, as in Hendry. Recorded from the 13th century.

Watson

Originally 'son of Wat', a diminutive of **Walter**. Recorded from the 15th century. George Watson (1654–1723) was an Edinburgh merchant who founded George Watson's College.

Watt

A diminutive of **Walter** recorded as a surname from the 15th century. James Watt (1736–1819) was the Scottish inventor of the pioneer steam engine.

Wauchope

From lands in Dumfriesshire. Recorded from the 13th century.

Waugh
From an abbreviation of **Wauchope**, recorded from the 13th century.

Wedderburn
From lands in Berwickshire, recorded as a surname from the 13th century.

Weir
From the Norman placenames of Vire and Vere. The aristocratic English surname De Vere is from the same source. Recorded in Scotland from the 12th century. Major Thomas Weir (1599–1670), captain of the Edinburgh town guard, was burnt for witchcraft.

Wells
An English name recorded in Scotland from c.1200, in Latin charters as de Fontibus.

Wellwood
From lands near Dunfermline in Fife. Recorded as a surname from the 15th century.

White, Whyte
A surname from an early nickname, like **Brown** and **Black**. Shown as Latin Albus in early records.

Whitelaw
From lands in the Borders, near Morebattle and also near Melrose. Recorded from the 13th century.

Wilkie, Willkie
From *Wil* or *Will+kie*, a double diminutive of **William**. Recorded from the 15th century. Sir David Wilkie (1785–1841) was a famous painter, of *Pitlessie Fair* (1804) among other subjects.

Williamson
Originally 'son of **William**', recorded from the 14th century. (See also **MacWilliam**.)

Wilson
Originally 'son of Wil', recorded from the 15th century. A popular medieval name in Scotland, after King William the Lion (1165–1214). Alexander Wilson (1766–1813) was a Scottish ornithologist in America, author of a seven-volume *American Ornithology* (1808–13). Charles Wilson (1869–1959) was a Scots nuclear physicist who shared a Nobel Prize (1927).

Wishart
From the Old-French name Guischard, 'wise, prudent'. Recorded from *c*.1200. George Wishart (*c*.1513–46) was a church reformer who was burnt at the stake for heresy at St Andrews – a precursor of the Reformation.

Witherspoon, Wotherspoon
The original etymology is uncertain, but it is likely that it had to do with *wethers*, or sheep in Old English. Recorded from the 15th century. John Witherspoon (1723–94) was a minister who went to America in 1768, and was a signatory of the Declaration of Independence.

Wright
Originally a wright was a person who 'wrought' or made things. In Scotland the name is recorded from the 13th century, and it came to mean a carpenter or joiner, neither of which names flourished as surnames north of the Border.

Wylie, Wyllie
Surnames from Willie, a diminutive of **William**. Recorded from the 14th century.

Yates
Originally indicated people who lived or worked at the *yate*, or gate. Recorded from the 14th century. Yeats and Yetts were alternative spellings.

Young, Younger
These names originally indicated the junior member of a household where two members bore the same Christian name. (Compare **Ogg**.) Young is recorded from the 13th century, Younger from the 14th. Young is now among the 20 most frequently found Scottish surnames. A possible alternative source for Younger is the Flemish name Joncker. James 'Paraffin' Young (1811–83) was a chemist whose experiments led to the commercial manufacture of paraffin oil

Yuill, Yool, Yell
Surnames of uncertain etymology, but perhaps from the forename Joel. Recorded from the 14th century. Yell is also a Shetland surname from the name of the island.